Corporate Acquisitions and Mergers in Serbia

Corporate Acquisitions and Mergers in Serbia

Fifth Edition

Milan Samardžić
Sara Ostojić
Mina Srećković
Stefan Savić
Tijana Kovačević
Nina Krunić
Jelisaveta Folić

Corporate/M&A Practice Group
Kinstellar Belgrade

Bojan Žepinić
Aleksandar Latinović
Jelena Hadžić
Ivana Rakočević
Ana Perović

Tax/Accounting Group TPA Serbia doo

This book was originally published as a chapter in Corporate Acquisitions and Mergers.

General Editor: Peter Begg

Wolters Kluwer

Published by:
Kluwer Law International B.V.
PO Box 316
2400 AH Alphen aan den Rijn
The Netherlands
E-mail: lrs-sales@wolterskluwer.com
Website: www.wolterskluwer.com/en/solutions/kluwerlawinternational

Sold and distributed by:
Wolters Kluwer Legal & Regulatory U.S.
920 Links Avenue
Landisville, PA 17538
United States of America
E-mail: customer.service@wolterskluwer.com

ISBN 978-94-035-3008-6

e-Book: ISBN 978-94-035-3018-5
web-PDF: ISBN 978-94-035-3028-4

Contents

Kinstellar Belgrade

SOG in cooperation with Kinstellar is a leading independent law firm in Emerging Europe, Turkey and Central Asia, with offices in Almaty and Nur-Sultan (Kazakhstan), Belgrade (Serbia), Bratislava (Slovakia), Bucharest (Romania), Budapest (Hungary), Istanbul (Turkey), Kyiv (Ukraine), Prague (the Czech Republic), Sofia (Bulgaria) and Tashkent (Uzbekistan).

Operating as a single fully integrated firm, Kinstellar delivers consistently high-quality services across all jurisdictions in an integrated and seamless style. We are particularly well suited to servicing complex transactions and advisory requirements spanning several jurisdictions. With offices in ten jurisdictions and over 180 local and international lawyers, we deliver consistent, cross-border legal advice and assistance across diverse regional markets.

Our clients include leading international and regional corporations, banks and other financial institutions, state bodies, multilateral institutions and international law firms with clients that require top-quality legal counsel in our jurisdictions. We handle important and complex assignments for clients across diverse industries and business sectors.

Kinstellar covers all aspects of domestic and international law, including Banking, Finance and Capital Markets, Competition and State Aid, Compliance, Risk and Sensitive Investigations, Dispute Resolution, Employment and Labour Law, Energy, Infrastructure and Projects, Intellectual Property (IP), Life Sciences and Healthcare, M&A and Corporate, Private Equity, Real Estate, Restructuring and Insolvency, Tax, Telecoms, Media and Technology.

TPA Serbia

TPA Serbia, as a part of the TPA Group, is a full-service tax advisory, accounting, auditing and financial advisory practice. The TPA Group is also present in the following countries in Central and South-Eastern Europe: Albania, Austria, Bulgaria, Croatia, Czech Republic, Hungary, Montenegro, Poland, Romania, Serbia, Slovakia and Slovenia with 1 700 staff members working at thirty locations.

The TPA Group is also an independent member of Baker Tilly Europe Alliance and is thus able to provide its clients with a worldwide network of tax advisors, auditors and consultants. Thanks to their alliance with the Baker Tilly International network, the twelve countries of the independent TPA Group are perfectly connected at a global level and able to provide high-quality services in all the main business centres and regions of the world. From its office in Belgrade, TPA Serbia renders services covering Serbia as well as Bosnia and Herzegovina.

Authors

This country chapter on Corporate M&A in the Republic of Serbia has been written by the following team of lawyers of Kinstellar Belgrade: *Milan Samardžić (Partner), Mina Srećković (Managing Associate), Sara Ostojić (Senior Associate), Stefan Savić (Senior Associate), Tijana Kovačević (Senior Associate), Nina Krunić (Associate) and Jelisaveta Folić (Associate).*

In addition to this, Chapters 4 (Taxation Aspects) and 6 (Accounting Treatment) have been written by the following members of the TPA Serbia team: Bojan Žepinić (Partner), Mirela Arsić (Senior Manager, Tax Department), Vesna Jovanović Pavlović (Consultant, Tax Department), Jelena Hadžić (Certified auditor) and Aleksandar Latinović (Assistant Manager, Audit Department)

SOG in cooperation with Kinstellar

Bulevar Mihaila Pupina 6/4, Ušće Tower 1, 11070 Novi Beograd

Serbia

Tel.: (381) 11 3210 200

Fax: (381) 11 3210 222

Website: www.kinstellar.com

TPA Tax and Accounting d.o.o. Makedonska 30 (Eurocentar), 3rd Floor 11000 Beograd

Serbia

Tel.: (381) 11 655 88 00

Fax: (381) 11 655 88 01

Website: www.tpa-group.rs

Disclaimer

Unless specified otherwise in the text, all references to applicable law and legislation as well as Euro (EUR) and Serbian Dinar (RSD) amounts are applicable as of 30 September 2023.

This document does not purport to contain a comprehensive summary of all the legal risks and issues in the legal areas it covers. It is to be used for information only and cannot be relied upon as legal advice, and no legal or business decision should be based solely on this document.

Definitions

Accounting Law means the Law on Accounting (Zakon o računovodstvu; Official Gazette of the Republic of Serbia, Nos 73/2019 and 44/2021).

Administrative Proceedings Law means the Law on General Administrative Proceedings (Zakon o opštem upravnom postupku; Official Gazette of the Republic of Serbia, Nos 18/2016, 95/2018 and 2/2023).

Agency Employment Law means the Law on Agency Employment (Zakon o agencijskom zapošljavanju; Official Gazette of the Republic of Serbia, No. 86/2019).

Anti-Corruption Agency means the Anti-Corruption Agency (Agencija za sprečavanje korupcije; www.acas.rs).

Articles of Association means the main corporate document of each joint-stock company, which sets out, *inter alia*, a corporate governance structure.

Association and Stabilization Treaty means Stabilization and Association Agreement (Sporazum o stabilizaciji i pridruživanju), an international treaty entered into force on 1 September 2013, granting the Republic of Serbia the status of an associated country to the European Union.

Banking Law means the Law on Banks (Zakon o bankama; Official Gazette of the Republic of Serbia, Nos 107/2005, 91/2010 and 14/2015).

BSA means the Bankruptcy Supervision Agency of Serbia (Agencija za licenciranje stečajnih upravnika; www.alsu.gov.rs).

Capital Markets Law means the Law on the Capital Market (Zakon o tržištu kapitala; Official Gazette of the Republic of Serbia, No 129/2021).

Central Register means the Central Securities Depository and Clearing House (Centralni registar, depo i kliring hartija od vrednosti; www.crhov.rs).

Company Law means the Law on Business Companies (Zakon o privrednim društvima; Official Gazette of the Republic of Serbia, Nos 36/2011, 99/2011, 83/2014, 5/2015, 44/2018, 95/2018, 91/2019, 109/2021).

Companies' Register means the register of companies maintained by the SBRA.

Competition Authority means the Commission for Protection of Competition of the Republic of Serbia (Komisija za zaštitu konkurencije Republike Srbije; www.kzk.org .rs).

Competition Law means the Law on the Protection of Competition (Zakon o zaštiti konkurencije; Official Gazette of the Republic of Serbia, Nos 51/2009 and 95/2013).

Corporate Income Tax Law means the Law on Corporate Income Tax (Zakon o porezu na dobit pravnih lica; Official Gazette of the Republic of Serbia, Nos 25/2001, 80/2002, 80/2002, 43/2003, 84/2004, 18/2010, 101/2011, 119/2012, 47/2013, 108/2013, 68/2014, 142/2014, 91/2015, 112/2015, 113/2017, 95/2018, 86/2019, 153/2020 and 118/2021).

Council Regulation (EC) No. 139/2004 means Council Regulation (EC) No. 139/2004 of 20 January 2004 on the control of concentrations between undertakings (the EC Merger Regulation).

Customs Tariff means Regulation on Harmonization of the Customs Tariff Nomenclature for 2023 (Uredba o usklađivanju nomenklature carinske tarife za 2023. godinu; Official Gazette of the Republic of Serbia, No. 132/2022 and 141/2022).

Decree means the Decree on the Content and Manner of Submission of the Request for Concentration (Uredba o sadržini i načinu podnošenja prijave koncentracije; Official Gazette of the Republic of Serbia, No. 5/2016).

EU means the European Union (www.europa.eu).

EUR means the official currency of the Eurozone.

Foreign Exchange Law means the Law on Foreign Exchange Operations (Zakon o deviznom poslovanju; Official Gazette of the Republic of Serbia, Nos 62/2006, 31/2011, 119/2012, 139/2014 and 30/2018).

Foundation Act means the constitutional document (deed of foundation) of a limited liability or a joint-stock company.

Insolvency Act means the Law on Insolvency (Zakon o stečaju; Official Gazette of the Republic of Serbia, Nos 104/2009, 99/2011, 71/2012, 83/2014, 113/2017, 44/2018 and 95/2018).

Insurance Law means the Law on Insurance (Zakon o osiguranju; Official Gazette of the Republic of Serbia, Nos 139/2014 and 44/2021).

Investment Law means the Law on Investments (Zakon o ulaganjima; Official Gazette of the Republic of Serbia, Nos 89/2015 and 95/2018).

IP Registers means registers of intellectual property maintained by the IPO.

IPO means the Intellectual Property Office of the Republic of Serbia (Zavod za intelektualnu svojinu Republike Srbije; www.zis.gov.rs).

Labour Law means the Law on Labour (Zakon o radu; Official Gazette of the Republic of Serbia, Nos 24/2005, 61/2005, 54/2009, 75/2014, 13/2017, 113/2017 and 95/2018).

Law on Agricultural Land means the Law on Agricultural Land (Zakon o poljoprivrednom zemljištu; Official Gazette of the Republic of Serbia, Nos 62/2006, 65/2008, 41/2009, 112/2015, 80/2017 and 95/2018).

Law on Alternative Investment Funds means the Law on Alternative Investment Funds (Zakon o alternativnim investicionim fondovima; Official Gazette of the Republic of Serbia, No. 73/2019).

Law on Central Register of Beneficial Owners means the Law on Central Register of Beneficial Owners (Zakon o centralnoj evidenciji stvarnih vlasnika; Official Gazette of the Republic of Serbia, Nos 41/2018, 91/2019, 105/2021 and 17/2023).

Law on Contracts and Torts means the Law on Contracts and Torts (Zakon o obligacionim odnosima; Official Gazette of the Socialist Federal Republic of Yugoslavia, Nos 29/78, 39/85, 45/89, 57/89, Official Gazette of the Federal Republic of Yugoslavia, No. 31/93; Official Gazette of Serbia and Montenegro, No. 1/2003; Official Gazette of the Republic of Serbia No. 18/2020).

Law on Digital Property means the Law on Digital Property (Zakon o digitalnoj imovini; Official Gazette of the Republic of Serbia, No. 153/2020).

Law on Employing Foreigners means the Law on Employing Foreigners (Zakon o zapošljavanju stranaca, Official Gazette of the Republic of Serbia, Nos 128/2014, 113/2017, 50/2018, 31/2019 and 62/2023).

Law on Employment and Insurance in Case of Unemployment means the Law on Employment and Insurance in Case of Unemployment (Zakon o zapošljavanju i osiguranju za slučaj nezaposlenosti; Official Gazette of the Republic of Serbia, Nos 36/2009, 88/2010, 38/2015, 113/2017, 113/2017 and 49/2021).

Law on Enforcement and Security means the Law on Enforcement and Security (Zakon o izvršenju i obezbeđenju; Official Gazette of the Republic of Serbia, Nos 106/2015, 106/2016, 113/2017, 54/2019, 9/2020 and 10/2023).

Law on Environmental Protection means the Law on Environmental Protection (Zakon o zaštiti životne sredine; Official Gazette of the Republic of Serbia, Nos 135/2004, 36/2009, 36/2009, 72/2009, 43/2011, 14/2016, 76/2018, 95/2018 and 95/2018).

Law on Open Investment Funds Subject to the Public Offer means the Law on Open Investment Funds Subject to the Public Offer (Zakon o otvorenim investicionim fondovima sa javnom ponudom; Official Gazette of the Republic of Serbia, No. 73/2019).

Law on Ownership and Other Property Rights means the Law on Ownership and Other Property rights (Zakon o osnovama svojinskopravnih odnosa; Official Gazette of the Socialist Federal Republic of Yugoslavia, Nos 6/80 and 36/90, Official Gazette of the Federal Republic of Yugoslavia No. 29/96 and Official Gazette of the Republic of Serbia, No. 115/2005).

Law on Pension and Disability Insurance means the Law on Pension and Disability Insurance (Zakon o penzijskom i invalidskom osiguranju; Official Gazette of the Republic of Serbia, Nos 34/2003, 64/2004, 84/2004, 85/2005, 101/2005, 63/2006, 5/2009, 107/2009, 101/2010, 93/2012, 62/2013, 108/2013, 75/2014, 142/2014, 73/2018, 46/2019, 86/2019, 62/2021, 125/2022, 138/2022 and 76/2023).

Law on Preventing Corruption means the Law on Preventing Corruption (Zakon o sprečavanju korupcije; Official Gazette of the Republic of Serbia, Nos 35/2019, 88/2019, 11/2021 and 14/2022).

Law on the Prevention of Money Laundering and Financing of Terrorism means the Law on the Prevention of Money Laundering and Financing of Terrorism (Zakon o sprečavanju pranja novca i finansiranja terorizma; Official Gazette of the Republic of Serbia, Nos 113/2017, 91/2019, 153/2020 and 92/2023).

Law on Protection of Right to a Trial within a Reasonable Time means the Law on Protection of Right to a Trial within a Reasonable Time (Zakon o zaštiti prava na suđenje u razumnom roku; Official Gazette of the Republic of Serbia, Nos 40/2015 and 92/2023).

Law on Public Notaries means the Law on Public Notaries (Zakon o javnom beležništvu; Official Gazette of the Republic of Serbia, Nos 31/2011, 85/2012, 19/2013, 55/2014, 93/2014, 121/2014, 6/2015 and 106/2015).

Law on the Protection of Business Secrets means the Law on the Protection of Business Secrets (Zakon o zaštiti poslovne tajne; Official Gazette of the Republic of Serbia, No. 53/2021).

Law on Protection of the Security and Health at Work means the Law on Protection of the Security and Health at Work (Zakon o bezbednosti i zdravlju na radu; Official Gazette of the Republic of Serbia, No 35/2023).

Law on Strike means the Law on Strike (Zakon o štrajku; Official Gazette of the Federal Republic of Yugoslavia No. 29/96 and Official Gazette of the Republic of Serbia, Nos 101/2005 and 103/2012).

Law on Use of the Renewable Energy Sources means the Law on Use of the Renewable Energy Sources (Zakon o korišćenju obnovljivih izvora energije; Official Gazette of the Republic of Serbia, Nos 40/2021 and 35/2023).

Mining Law means the Law on Mining and Geological Explorations (Zakon o rudarstvu i geološkim istraživanjima; Official Gazette of the Republic of Serbia, Nos 101/2015, 95/2018 and 40/2021).

Ministry of Finance means the Ministry of Finance of the Republic of Serbia (Ministarstvo finansija Republike Srbije; www.mfin.gov.rs).

Ministry of Interior means the Ministry of Interior of the Republic of Serbia (Ministarstvo unutrašnjih poslova Republike Srbije; www.mup.gov.rs).

Ministry of Labour means the Ministry of Labour, Employment, Social Affair and Veterans of the Republic of Serbia (Ministarstvo za rad, zapošljavanje, boračka i socijalna pitanja Republike Srbije; www.minrzs.gov.rs).

Mortgage Law means the Mortgage Law (Zakon o hipoteci; Official Gazette of the Republic of Serbia, Nos 115/2005, 60/2015, 63/2015 and 83/2015).

National Health Insurance Fund means the Republic Health Insurance Fund (Republički fond za zdravstveno osiguranje; www.rfzo.rs).

National Labor Authority means the National Service for Employment of the Republic of Serbia (Nacionalna služba za zapošljavanje Republike Srbije; www.nsz.gov.rs).

NBS means the National Bank of Serbia (Narodna banka Srbije; www.nbs.rs).

OECD Transfer Pricing Guidelines means the Transfer Pricing Guidelines for Multinational Enterprises and Tax Administrations approved by the OECD Council.

Personal Income Tax Law means the Law on Personal Income Tax (Zakon o porezu na dohodak građana; Official Gazette of the Republic of Serbia, Nos 24/2001,

80/2002, 80/2002, 135/2004, 62/2006, 65/2006, 31/2009, 44/2009, 18/2010, 50/2011, 91/2011, 7/2012, 93/2012, 114/2012, 8/2013, 47/2013, 48/2013, 108/2013, 6/2014, 57/2014, 68/2014, 5/2015, 112/2015, 5/2016, 7/2017, 113/2017, 7/2018, 95/2018, 4/2019, 86/2019, 5/2020, 153/2020, 156/2020, 6/2021, 44/2021, 118/2021, 132/2021, 10/2022, 138/2022, 144/2022, 6/2023 and 92/2023).

Pledge Law means the Law on Pledge on Movable Assets and Rights Registered in the Pledge Registry (Zakon o založnom pravu na pokretnim stvarima upisanim u registar; Official Gazette of the Republic of Serbia, Nos 57/2003, 61/2005, 64/2006 and 99/2011 and 31/2019).

Pledge Register means the Register of Pledges on Movable Property and Rights maintained by the SBRA.

RAS means the Development Agency of Serbia (Razvojna agencija Srbije; ras.gov.rs).

Real Estate Register means the land cadaster maintained by the RGA.

Register of Financial Statements is the register of financial statements maintained by the SBRA.

RGA means the Republic Geodetic Authority (Republički geodetski zavod; www.rgz.gov.rs).

RSD means Serbian Dinar, being the lawful currency of Serbia.

SBRA means Serbian Business Registries Agency (Agencija za privredne registre Republike Srbije), a governmental agency competent for operating various types of commercial registries in Serbia.

SEC means the Securities Commission of the Republic of Serbia (Komisija za hartije od vrednosti Republike Srbije; www.sec.gov.rs).

Serbia means the Republic of Serbia (Republika Srbija).

Serbian Government means the Government of the Republic of Serbia (Vlada Republike Srbije).

SPA means a share purchase agreement.

Stock Exchange means the Belgrade Stock Exchange (Beogradska berza; www.belex.rs).

Takeover Law means the Law on Takeover of Joint-Stock Companies (Zakon o preuzimanju akcionarskih društava; Official Gazette of the Republic of Serbia, Nos 46/2006, 107/2009, 99/2011 and 108/2016).

Transfer Pricing Rulebook means the Rulebook on Transfer Pricing and Methods Which Are Applied At 'Arm's Length' Principle in Determining the Price of Transactions Between Related Parties (Pravilnik o transfernim cenama i metodama koje se po principu 'van dohvata ruke' primenjuju kod utvrđivanja cene transakcija među povezanim licima; Official Gazette of the Republic of Serbia, Nos 61/2013, 8/2014, 94/2019 and 95/2021).

VAT means value added tax.

VAT Law means the Law on Value Added Tax (Zakon o porezu na dodatu vrednost; Official Gazette of the Republic of Serbia, Nos 84/2004, 86/2004, 61/2005, 61/2007, 93/2012, 108/2013, 6/2014, 68/2014, 142/2014, 5/2015, 83/2015, 5/2016, 108/2016, 7/2017, 113/2017, 13/2018, 30/2018, 4/2019, 72/2019, 8/2020, 153/2020 and 138/2022).

Work Inspectorate means the Work Inspectorate within the Ministry of Labor and Social Policy of Serbia (Inspektorat za rad; www.minrzs.gov.rs).

1 LOCAL ECONOMIC, POLITICAL AND CULTURAL ASPECTS

1.1 Geographic Location

[01] Serbia lies at the crossroads of Central and Eastern Europe and has historical, political and cultural, as well as economic and commercial ties with its neighbouring countries. It borders European Union (EU) states at the Croatian, Hungarian, Bulgarian, and Romanian state borders while at the same time maintaining historically good relations with Russia and the countries of the Middle East.

1.2 Infrastructure

[02] In terms of infrastructure, Serbia is very well connected with both Western and Eastern countries via two pan-European corridors which intersect its territory – corridor No. 7 (along the River Danube) and corridor No. 10 (which connects Salzburg and Thessaloniki). In addition to this, in 2010, Serbia began developing its portion of the so-called corridor 11 from Belgrade to the port of Bar in Montenegro, which is part of a longer route planned to connect Timisoara in Romania and Bari in Italy. In late 2019, the part of corridor 11 named 'Miloš Veliki Highway' was opened for traffic. The motorway network has been continually expanding as several large projects have been announced and/or launched, including the construction of the Moravian Corridor, the Fruškogorski Corridor, the Niš-Pločnik Motorway and several other motorways.

[03] The railway network is fairly well developed but, in most parts, outdated; due to this reason, the average speed of trains is far below European standards. In light of this, one of the most important ongoing projects is the modernization and reconstruction of the Belgrade–Budapest railway which was developed by the Serbian and Hungarian governments and supported by Chinese funds. In addition, in March 2021, the World Bank approved the initial phase of the Multi-Phase Programmatic Approach for Serbia Railway Sector Modernization Project, the aim of which is to renew and modernize the railway network.

[04] Serbia offers outstanding potential for river transportation. The Danube and the Sava (both international rivers) represent major navigable routes which can be used for transportation throughout the year.

1.3 Natural Resources

[05] Besides having substantial potential in renewable energy resources, including water, wind, solar and biomass, Serbia is also endowed with certain other natural resources, such as coal, copper, iron ore, lead, zinc, lithium, nickel and cobalt, which have considerable potential for exploration and exploitation.

1.4 Population

[06] According to the latest statistics for 2022, Serbia has 6 664 449 citizens (excluding Kosovo). The majority of its citizens are Serbs, with a number of national minorities. The Serbian language is the official language of the country, while national minorities are allowed to use their language in official correspondence and proceedings with governmental bodies in accordance with the law (i.e., national minorities who represent at least 2% of the total population in Serbia may use their language in official correspondence and proceedings with governmental bodies).

[07] According to some sources, the estimated population growth rate in 2020 was negative (i.e., -6.7%), and the median age of the Serbian population is 43.4 years.

1.5 Employment Costs and Availability of Labour

[08] According to official sources in Serbia, the unemployment rate in the third quarter of 2023 was 9.0%. Further, the gross average salary in September 2023 on the Republic of Serbia level amounted to RSD117 472 (approximately EUR1 000), and the net salary (gross salary minus applicable taxes) on the Republic of Serbia level amounts to RSD85 066 (approximately EUR720).

[09] Many people have opened their own business operations as entrepreneurs in the last twenty years of economic transition in Serbia. However, due to the relatively heavy burden of applicable taxes and social and other contributions, a lack of low-interest financing, as well as other unfavourable conditions, many such entrepreneurs have been forced to close their operations within a short space of time. Consequently, Serbia still has a relatively large number of people who make their living in the so-called grey economy trading in goods and services outside of the official cash flows.

1.6 Government and Political System

[10] Since 2000, Serbia has actively promoted policies which encourage foreign direct investment (FDI) and the country's accession to the EU. On 1 March 2012, Serbia was awarded the status of an EU candidate country. The main open political issue which dominates the Serbian foreign policy agenda and has had an increased bearing on Serbia's aspirations towards EU accession is the situation related to Kosovo. Kosovo proclaimed its independence from Serbia in 2008, but this move has not been recognized by Serbia and a number of other states. In 2013, the EU approved Serbia for negotiations for membership after Serbia and Kosovo participated in talks aimed at the normalization of their relationships, and in December 2015, Serbia opened negotiation chapters with the EU. Out of the total number of thirty-five chapters, eighteen chapters have been opened until mid-2021, while two chapters have been temporarily closed.

[11] Accession to the EU remains high on the political agenda of the current Serbian Government bearing in mind the further harmonization of the domestic laws with the laws of the EU and increasing efforts to liberalize the market and bring more foreign investors to the country by means of offering various incentives (please *see* paragraphs **[72]–[89]** for more information on the treatment of foreign investors in Serbia). However, the major assets of the country, such as the national telecommunications company Telekom Srbija, national electric power producer Elektroprivreda Srbije, and national railway company Železnice Srbije remain wholly state-owned and controlled. Although recent reports suggest that the Government is considering privatizing in part or entirely some of the aforementioned and other similar state-owned companies, it is yet to be seen whether and how this will unfold in the period to come.

1.7 Integration into Global Financial System

[12] Even though it is outside the so-called Eurozone, Serbia appears to be fairly well integrated into the global financial system. For example, in order to prepare itself for the transition into the European system of central banks, the National Bank of Serbia (NBS) has already adopted various standards used by the European Central Bank. In addition, the Serbian banking market is dominated by foreign banks, which have also brought to the market some internationally recognized standards. As a part of its efforts to join the World Trade Organization, Serbia has made an effort to further liberalize its financial regulations. However, the rules stipulated by the Foreign Exchange Law (despite having been amended on several occasions in the recent period) and its quite conservative interpretation by the NBS still represent an obstacle to the uninterrupted movement of foreign currency across the border.

1.8 Membership in International Trade and Political Associations

[13] Serbia is a member of the main global political organizations, such as the United Nations, the Organisation for Security and Co-operation in Europe, and the Council of Europe, and is an associate member of the EU. However, negotiations regarding its accession to the World Trade Organization are still ongoing.

[14] From a regional perspective, it is important to point out that Serbia is a member of the Central European Free Trade Association (CEFTA), which was established pursuant to the trade agreement signed between Albania, Bosnia and

Herzegovina, North Macedonia, Moldova, Montenegro, Serbia and the United Nations Interim Administration Mission (UNMIK) in Kosovo. This agreement took effect in July 2007 and represents an important export tool for companies based in Serbia.

[15] Furthermore, Serbia has concluded a number of treaties that enable the customs-free trade of goods that originate in Serbia, such as the Association and Stabilisation Treaty with the EU, free trade agreements with the Russian Federation, Turkey, Belarus and Kazakhstan, as well as an agreement with the European Free Trade Association (EFTA) Member States (Switzerland, Norway, Iceland and Liechtenstein).

1.9 Legal System

[16] Serbia is a civil law jurisdiction and is in the process of harmonizing its laws with the EU *acquis*. Therefore, the general legal framework of Serbia will not be totally unfamiliar to legal practitioners and business persons who are used to working in the civil law jurisdictions of the EU. At the same time, the country continues to retain features of the legal system which are particular to Serbia.

[17] The Serbian Government has attempted to speed up the process of harmonization with the EU laws. However, a number of newly adopted laws lack implementing legislation and clear guidance on their application. Such lack of clarity represents a major obstacle to the efficient interpretation and application of new rules. Moreover, obtaining effective and timely legal protection from the Serbian courts remains one of the most-recognized current shortcomings of the Serbian judicial system and the country as a whole (*see* paragraphs **[145]–[155]** for more information on the role of the courts in Serbia).

1.10 Identifying Acquisition Targets

[18] In the context of the private sector, one of the most practical ways to identify potential acquisition targets in Serbia is to contact various professional services providers, such as consulting companies, law firms and the Big 4 international accounting firms, who often have information on the relevant 'offer' and 'demand' in this context.

[19] In the public sector, the Ministry of Commerce can offer various information on the companies that are undergoing privatization and, as such, are in the portfolio of this body. Also, the Development Agency of Serbia (RAS), the main role of which is to attract foreign investment in the country and assist foreign investors in the process, can assist in identifying potential green and brown-field opportunities.

1.11 Current Economic Aspects

[20] The first half of 2020 was marked by the COVID-19 crisis, as the global pandemic negatively affected the economic activity in Serbia, starting from March 2020, when the state of emergency was declared. However, the investments resumed as of July in the sectors that were not only unaffected by the pandemic but also seemed to prosper during the pandemic, such as fast-moving consumer goods (FMCG), IT, pharmaceutical and home care products.

[21] The dominant trend in the market for provision of financial services, which is the banking market consolidation, continued in 2020 with the acquisition of direct controlling ownership in Komercijalna banka a.d. Beograd from the Republic of Serbia by one of the largest Slovenian banks – Nova Ljubljanska banka d.d. Ljubljana and the ongoing process of integration (in the form of merger) of its two subsidiaries in the Serbian market, i.e., NLB Banka a.d. Beograd and Komercijalna banka a.d. Beograd. In addition, Opportunity International completed the sale of 78% of Opportunity Bank Serbia (OBS), Opportunity International's banking operations in Serbia, to a consortium of European values-driven financial institutions, while Raiffeisen Bank Serbia acquired 100% of Credit Agricole Serbia. Finally, a merger between Eurobank Serbia and Direktna Banka Serbia was completed on 13 December 2021.

[22] According to some sources, the GDP growth rate was nominally higher at 13.2% in relation to the previous year and realistically was higher at 2.5%. The International Monetary Fund (IMF) predicts that Serbia's economy will grow by 2% in 2023.[1]

1.12 Main Industries and Trends

[23] The key industries in Serbia are traditionally agriculture, automobiles, telecommunications, base metals, oil, gas, furniture, food processing, machinery, chemicals, tyres, clothes and pharmaceuticals. However, there is an increasing number of investments in the tourism, real estate, energy, automotive and IT sectors. Foreign investors are generally free to invest in these industries on the same terms as Serbian nationals. In this respect, it is worth mentioning that many of the main market players in these sectors are large international corporations, such as Fiat, Michelin, Stada, Coca-Cola, Gazprom and Telenor. Additionally, Kyungshin Cable Europe, a Korean company, completed construction and officially opened its factory for the production of parts for car batteries in the industrial zone of Smederevska Palanka in 2020. Further, Chinese Yanfeng and American Adient opened factories in Kragujevac and Loznica to manufacture automotive interior parts.

[1] https://seenews.com/news/imf-maintains-serbias-2-2023-gdp-growth-fcast-836316.

[24] The only formal restriction in the context of the aforementioned industries relates to agriculture, where ownership of agricultural land is still reserved for Serbian nationals unless otherwise determined in accordance with the Association and Stabilisation Treaty. Under the amended Law on Agricultural Land, EU citizens are required to live in Serbia for at least ten years before purchasing land, with plot sizes limited to two hectares. They should farm land as a lessee for at least three years before buying it, and a seller must first offer it to the state. The rules prohibit the sale of land close to military facilities and in national parks. However, in practice, this obstacle is frequently avoided by the inclusion of Serbian companies in the ownership chain and is most of the time tolerated by relevant authorities.

[25] Investment strategies differ depending on the industry sector. However, there is increasing activity on the part of both private equity funds and the main international financial institutions, such as the European Bank for Reconstruction and Development (EBRD). The latter has been particularly active in Serbia not only in infrastructure financing and other similar public sector projects but also in taking minority ownership in private companies in various sectors, and so far, the EBRD has invested approximately EUR5.1 bn in the country. Also, there is visible activity in the market for sale of non-performing loans of both portfolios held by banks and private companies. Finally, as mentioned above, privatization of the major state-controlled Komercijalna banka took place in 2020.

[26] Recent activities in the sector of renewable energy, i.e., adoption of a new law governing renewables, which may indicate an investment trend in the following years, demonstrate an increased interest of foreign investors in the development and acquisition of renewable power plants. Currently, there are nine wind farms in Serbia which are in the operation phase, with a total installed capacity of approximately 400 MW, which operational wind farms received feed-in tariffs in line with the previously applicable legal framework, which was applicable until 31 December 2019. In line with the request from the Energy Community Secretariat, at the beginning of 2021, the Serbian Government decided to start to develop an auction-based incentives model, which is already in place at some other members of the Energy Community, such as North Macedonia, Albania and Montenegro. The new regulatory framework which includes, *inter alia,* adoption of a brand new Law on Use of the Renewable Energy Sources came into force on 30 April 2021. However, by-laws necessary for the implementation of the Law on Use of the Renewable Energy Sources, especially one governing auctions, have not yet been adopted. According to the transitional and closing provisions of the Law on Use of the Renewable Energy Sources, by-laws are supposed to be adopted within six months of the entry into force of the said law (i.e., by 30 October 2021), which they were and are currently duly applicable.

[27] It is also relevant to note that the new Law on Digital Property, which entered into force on 29 June 2021, has set forth the legal framework for the area of digital property and provided additional space for the development of the capital market as well as the opportunities for investment into digital assets. The Law on Digital

Property governs the issuance and secondary trading of digital assets in the Republic of Serbia, provision of digital asset services, pledge and fiduciary rights on digital assets, as well as the competencies of the SEC and the NBS as supervisory bodies over the application of the relevant rules.

1.13 Main Foreign Investors' Rights and Considerations

[28] In general, Serbian law stipulates equal rights and obligations for both Serbian and foreign legal entities. A foreign investor is guaranteed 'national treatment', which means that any legal entity or natural person that is investing in Serbia enjoys full legal security and protection equal to that of domestic companies.

[29] Establishing a business in Serbia is quite simple and inexpensive and normally takes from three to five business days from the date of the filing of the relevant documentation with the Companies' Register. The minimum registered capital required for a limited liability company (which is the most common vehicle used by investors) is as little as RSD100 (currently approximately EUR0.80).

[30] However, in certain more regulated sectors, foreign investors may face difficulties in dealing with regulatory bodies as there is no 'one-stop-shop' system for obtaining all the necessary licences/approvals, which may lead to delays in the process of completing such projects. Nevertheless, introduction of the so-called unified system for obtaining construction permits within 28 days, instead of the previous average of 240 days, represents a major step forward in expediting the overall permitting procedure. To the best of our knowledge, this deadline is generally complied with in practice by the competent authorities. Further weak points of the current legal system, such as the aforementioned lack of practice in the application of newly adopted laws designed to comply with the EU regulations and the uncertain legal practice of regulatory bodies, appear to be a common feature of emerging economies, which may be well controlled and mitigated with the assistance of competent advisors.

1.14 Business Culture

[31] Business culture in Serbia is, in many respects, similar to other countries in its region. Therefore, informed foreign businessmen will recognize that western business values have been accepted in Serbia for many years. Much less formal standards of behaviour and longer business meetings (which often continue over lunch) are distinctive features of Serbian business, which may sometimes come as a surprise to some foreigners. However, the business culture has suffered significant changes due to the COVID-19 pandemic, as meetings were predominantly held remotely.

[32] Giving and receiving gifts of symbolic value is customary around holiday seasons and as part of a company's efforts to present itself. However, when choosing an appropriate gift, one must pay attention to the applicable statutory limits for the value of such gifts. Also, many companies have their own internal rules for assessing what may be given as a present in business relationships.

2 THE REGULATORY FRAMEWORK

2.1 Business Vehicles

2.1.1 Available Corporate Forms

[33] The following main corporate forms are available in Serbia: limited liability company (*društvo sa ograničenom odgovornošću* or *d.o.o.*); joint-stock company (*akcionarsko društvo* or *a.d.*); partnership (*ortačko društvo* or *o.d.*); and limited partnership (*komanditno društvo* or *k.d.*). In addition, entrepreneurs (*preduzetnici*) are entitled to carry out business activities as natural persons. There are other types of legal entities which are less relevant from the point of view of foreign investors, *inter alia*, public enterprises (*javna preduzeća or j.p.*), state-owned and state-run entities which perform commercial activities declared as being of public interest, e.g., supplying utilities managing power grids, institutions *(ustanove)* as entities constituted for performance of activities in areas of education, healthcare and social welfare and business associations (*poslovna udruženja*) as non-profitable entities established solely for achieving common interests of their members.

[34] In addition, the amendments of the Company Law adopted in 2018, as a part of the process of aligning Serbian law with the EU laws, introduced two additional forms of legal entities: European joint-stock company (*Evropsko akcionarsko društvo (Societas Europea) or s.e.)*, a joint-stock company incorporated in Serbia by way of a merger of, or entering into a holding or joint venture arrangement by, at least, one Serbian and one EU company, or by a change of legal form of a Serbian joint-stock company which has a controlled company in an EU member country; and European economic interest group (*Evropska ekonomska interesna grupacija or EEIG*), a non-profit legal entity incorporated in Serbia by, at least, one Serbian and one EU company or entrepreneur, for easier achieving, developing, complying and representing commercial and other interests of their members in Serbia and EU.

[35] Foreign entities can conduct business in Serbia via a branch or through incorporation of or participation in Serbian entities. Foreign entities may also establish their representative offices in Serbia but such entities may only conduct preparatory and research activities that lead to the conclusion of specific commercial arrangements and cannot undertake such commercial obligations in their own name (i.e., this right is reserved for their foreign parents). However, they are allowed to conclude arrangements which are related to their everyday business activities, and their foreign parents shall be deemed liable for all obligations stipulated in such arrangements.

2.1.2 Companies' Register and Central Register of Beneficial Owners

[36] All companies are required to be registered in the Companies' Register. Registration with the Companies' Register normally takes up to five business days from the date of the filing of the relevant documentation. A company is deemed to exist and may commence business activities upon registration with the Companies' Register. Some of the information that is filed within the Companies' Register is accessible over the Internet website of the 'Serbian Business Registries Agency (SBRA) (www.apr.gov.rs), which is the agency in charge of Companies' Register and a number of other official registries (the Pledge Register, the Financial Reports Register, the Financial Leasing Register, etc.). Although the information available on the SBRA website is generally reliable, such information should be verified by an original extract (hard copy) from the Companies' Register, as this is the only official information source on a company in Serbia. Additionally, the incorporation of certain forms of a company (limited liability company, joint-stock company, partnership and limited partnership) is conducted solely electronically starting from 17 May 2023 via the official platform and application form of the SBRA by using the qualified electronic signature of an authorized person to file a registration application.

[37] The constitutive documents and financial statements of companies are filed with the SBRA and are accessible to the general public at the Companies' Register and the Register of Financial Statements, respectively.

[38] In addition, the Law on Central Register of Beneficial Owners provides an obligation for all Serbian legal entities, including companies, to register their beneficial owners with the Central Register of Beneficial Owners. In accordance with this law, a beneficial owner is any natural person who owns 25% or more in the equity of a legal entity, or a natural person who has a prevailing influence on business activities of a legal entity, or a natural person who finances activities of a legal entity and thus significantly influences the decision-making process, or a natural person who is a founder, trustee, beneficiary or has a dominant position in a trust or other foreign legal entity. In case the beneficial owner of a legal entity cannot be determined following any of the aforementioned criteria, the statutory representative of a legal entity should be considered its beneficial owner. Additionally, business entities incorporated in the Republic of Serbia are obliged to perform the registration of an ultimate beneficial owner within fifteen calendar days from incorporation, i.e., any change thereof and such registration is done via qualified electronic signature of a company's director (such qualified electronic signature is obtained from one of the certification bodies in Serbia and the director's, i.e., representatives of entities use it for filing annual financial statements).

2.1.3 Most Common Company Types and Ownership Structure

[39] The most common company form in Serbia is a limited liability company, followed by a joint-stock company.

[40] As far as ownership structure is concerned, generally, both limited liability companies and joint-stock companies may have a sole member/shareholder, but joint-stock companies typically have more than one shareholder. Also, certain businesses can be formed only in the form of a joint-stock company (e.g., banks, insurance companies):

(1) Limited Liability Company:

(a) Basic Characteristics

A limited liability company is the vehicle generally used in situations where there are a limited number of investors who plan to hold their investments in the company for the medium to long term. A limited liability company is typically used for small to medium-sized enterprises. A limited liability company may be founded by one or more members (i.e., shareholder(s) of a limited liability company), who may be natural or legal persons. The Company Law does not prescribe the maximum number of members. The founders established a limited liability company by the execution of a foundation act (*osnivački akt*) and its registration within the Companies' Register. The shareholders of a limited liability company may conclude a members' agreement (i.e., shareholders agreement) which binds only those shareholders of the company who concluded it. The Company Law does not prescribe mandatory elements of such shareholders' agreement in the same manner as it prescribes mandatory elements of a foundation act.

(b) Registered Capital:

The minimum basic capital required for the registration of a limited liability company is RSD100 (approximately EUR0.80) unless otherwise provided by a specific regulation, e.g., if an insurance broker company is incorporated in the form of a limited liability company, its minimum basic capital may not be below the amounts in euros which are prescribed by the newly introduced Capital Markets Law, calculated in RSD equivalent pursuant to the middle exchange rate of the NBS. The registered capital of a limited liability company is divided into ownership interests (*udeli*), whereas each member can hold only one ownership interest at a time in one company. As a general rule, value of the shareholder's contribution to the company's capital against total contribution of all shareholders corresponds with the percentage of the ownership interest in the total registered basic capital. However, at the time of a company's foundation or, subsequently, pursuant to a unanimous decision by the company's general assembly, the company's members may set the size of ownership interests in a manner that is not proportionate to the value of their related capital contribution. Such discrepancy in proportions needs to be stated in the foundation act of a company or a decision of a shareholders' assembly.

Co-ownership of an ownership interest in a limited liability company is possible and is exercised by a joint proxy, which represents all co-owners who are jointly liable for exercise of their rights. An ownership interest carries the rights and duties of each member, in particular, voting rights and rights to dividends which are (unless otherwise stipulated in the company's foundation act) in direct proportion to the member's contribution to the company's total registered basic capital.

Limited liability companies may not issue the equivalent of preference shares. However, similar results can be achieved by altering default statutory rights attaching to ownership interests.

In addition, following amendments to the Company Law, which came into force on 1 January 2020, limited liability companies may reserve a part of their ownership interest by transforming it into a treasury ownership interest, issuing a financial instrument of right to acquire ownership interest (*pravo na sticanje udela*) in the percentage of such transformed treasury ownership interest, and registering such financial instrument with the Central Register. Registered financial instrument entitles its holder to acquire a certain percentage of ownership interest in a limited liability company under pre-defined conditions. The idea behind this is to motivate important employees of a limited liability company with the possibility of acquiring a part of the stake in the limited liability company in case certain conditions are met. In relation to it, it should be noted that a decision on transforming the ownership interest and issuing a financial instrument requires a two-thirds majority of votes in the general assembly of the company, whereas only the ownership interest of members who voted to adopt this decision may be transformed.

As in most jurisdictions, members are not personally liable for the company's obligations, with some limited exceptions.

The registered basic capital of a limited liability company and the capital contributions of individual members are recorded in the Companies' Register. Any changes to the registered capital must be approved by the two-thirds majority of the general assembly of the relevant company (unless a different majority, but not lower than the simple majority of all members, is provided by the foundation act) and recorded in the Companies' Register. It should be noted that a decision on decrease of the basic capital of a limited liability company may be reached only in certain cases – i.e., only if such decrease is required to cover losses of the company or to establish or increase reserves of the company for covering future losses or increase of the basic capital from net assets of the company, or in case of annulment of the member's ownership interest or company's own ownership interest. In addition, a decision on decrease of basic capital must be registered with the Companies' Register within three months after it was reached, and it remains published on the Internet website of the SBRA for a period of an additional three months from the day of its registration, allowing the company's creditors to seek adequate collaterals for their receivables from the company. Contributions to the registered capital of a limited liability company can be in the form of cash or in-kind contributions. However, even in the case of in-kind contributions, such contributions must be expressed in the equivalent amount of cash denominated in RSD. An in-kind contribution can be made in the form of an asset and/or a right. The value of an in-kind contribution is determined either on the basis of the shareholders' agreement or on the basis of a formal valuation made by an expert who is authorized by the competent authority to undertake valuations of that particular asset and/or right and appointed as such by the company's shareholders. Such valuation cannot be older than one year as of the day on which the contribution is made and it should be registered with the Companies' Register.

(c) Corporate Governance

A limited liability company may have a one- or two-tier corporate governance structure. In the case of a one-tier corporate governance structure, corporate bodies of a limited liability company are the general assembly and one or more directors. In the event that a limited liability company has a two-tier corporate governance structure, corporate bodies are the general assembly, supervisory board and one or more directors. A company's foundation act shall determine which of these two models of corporate governance will be applied in each individual limited liability company.

In the case of the one-tier corporate governance structure, the directors must be appointed and relieved by the general assembly, while in the case a company has a two-tier corporate governance structure, the supervisory board shall appoint and relieve the directors and supervise their work, whereas members of the supervisory board shall be appointed, supervised and relieved by the general assembly. The number of directors is determined either by the foundation act or by the general assembly decision and in any moment a company must have at least one director. Appointment of directors and members of the supervisory board, if applicable, is subject to the mandatory registration with the Companies' Registry. However, the registration with the Companies' Register is of declarative nature; thus, the directors, i.e., members of a supervisory board, are considered appointed at the moment of rendering a decision on appointment by the competent body in a company.

In the event that a company has two or more directors, they represent the company towards third parties jointly and without limitations unless the company's foundation act or general assembly decision provides otherwise. However, irrespective of any possible limitations to directors' representation powers, the Company Law provides that any undertaking of will made towards one director is deemed to have been duly made towards the company. The general rule from the Company Law is that the limitations in directors' representations cannot be imposed on third parties, unless such limitation is duly registered in the Companies' Register.

The Company Law also defines the competencies of a limited liability company's directors very broadly: all the competencies that do not represent competencies of the general assembly (in the one-tier corporate governance model) or the general assembly and supervisory board (in the two-tier corporate governance model). In practice, this means that directors are in charge of, *inter alia*, a company's representation and management of its day-to-day affairs. Additionally, a director is liable for proper management of a company's business books and accuracy of financial statements.

(d) Other Important Issues
A limited liability company may appoint one or more persons to be in charge of the internal control/audit of the company's business activities. In such case, the company in question may provide in its foundation act which particular qualifications (if any) such person should have.

(2) Joint-Stock Company:

(a) Basic Characteristics and Foundation:
The Company Law regulates joint-stock companies in the general sense of the term but also provides for special, somewhat stricter rules for the so-called public joint-stock companies, which are not precisely defined by the Company Law. However, pursuant to the Capital Markets Law, public joint-stock companies are defined as an issuer: (i) that has successfully completed a public offer of securities in accordance with a prospectus whose publication was approved by the Securities Commission of Serbia (SEC), or (ii) whose securities are admitted to trading on the regulated market/multilateral trading platform (MTP) or organized trading platform (OTP). MTP is defined as a multilateral system which is organized and/or operated by a market organizer or investment company and which, within the system and in accordance with binding rules, connects offers to buy and offers to sell financial instruments from several interested third parties in a way that leads to the conclusion of a contract, in accordance with the Capital Markets Law. OTP is defined as a multilateral system that is not a regulated market or MTP, within which offers for the purchase and offers for the sale of bonds, structured financial products, emission units or derivative financial instruments of several interested third parties are connected, in a way that leads to the conclusion of a contract in accordance with the Capital Markets Law.

A joint-stock company may be founded pursuant to a public call for subscription and purchase of its shares. However, this is not currently common in Serbia, where typically, the initial founders establish a joint-stock company, which can subsequently make public offers for subscription and purchase of its shares for the purpose of securing additional capital for the company. A joint-stock company may have an unlimited number of founders/shareholders and is thus the company form generally used for larger businesses.

At the time of the incorporation of a joint-stock company, its founders execute the company's foundation act and the first articles of association. The company will legally exist from the date of registration with the Companies' Register. Subsequently, the foundation act of a joint-stock company cannot be amended. Instead, all the relevant changes (e.g., changes to the corporate governance structure) are made through amendments to the company's articles of association.

(b) Registered Capital and Shares

The registered capital of joint-stock companies is divided into a certain number of shares with a specified nominal value. Under Company Law, the minimum registered basic capital for each joint-stock company is RSD3 m (approximately EUR25 400). However, certain types of businesses have different minimal registered basic capital requirements (such as banks, which have the prescribed minimum registered monetary basic capital of EUR10 m).

A joint-stock company may issue ordinary shares and preference shares. Preference shares may be divided into two or more share classes (i.e., in the case of multiple share classes, such classes differ in the rights they accord to their shareholders). However, ordinary shares may only comprise one share class (i.e., they always confer the same rights).

Shares can be issued with or without nominal value. In case shares are issued with nominal value, all the shares of the same class must have the same nominal value, while the minimum nominal value of each share is RSD100 (approximately EUR0.80). The nominal value of shares is determined by a decision on their issuance. The nominal value of a company's preference shares cannot be lower than the nominal value of its ordinary shares.

The typical preference share rights include rights such as preference over ordinary shares in dividend distributions and priority in distribution in the event of the company's liquidation. The total nominal value of the issued and authorized preference shares may not exceed one-half of the company's registered basic capital, and they can be issued only against a monetary contribution to the basic capital of a company.

Any share issued by a joint-stock company must be approved by the SEC and subsequently registered (along with all the details pertaining to the respective shareholder) with the Central Register. A shareholder is a natural or legal person who/that is registered as such in the Central Register.

A joint-stock company is obliged to register a decision on the increase of registered basic capital within six months from the date of the adoption of such decision determining, *inter alia*, the amount of the increase and deadlines for registration of potential acquirers of new shares. In order for increase of basic capital by monetary payments to be successful, registered potential acquirers of shares have to, immediately upon the expiration of the registration deadline, pay at least one-quarter of the nominal or accounting value of the newly registered shares which increase their part of the share capital, whereas the remaining part may be paid in the period of five years since the registration of the decision on the increase (two years in case of public joint-stock companies) unless a shorter deadline is provided by a decision on increase. In case of increase of basic capital by way of in-kind contributions, such contributions have to be entered into a joint-stock company in full within a period of five years since the registration of the decision on the increase (two years in case of public joint-stock companies) unless a shorter deadline is provided by a decision on increase.

With respect to a decision on a decrease in registered basic capital, such a decision must be reached by the three-quarters majority of present shareholders in each class of shares that has voting rights in relation to this issue and must be registered within three months from the date of its adoption. Decrease of the registered basic capital can be performed by withdrawal and annulment of shareholder's shares (if previously provided by articles of association prior to registration of shares in question, or if all shareholders affected by this withdrawal reach a consensus on this), annulment of company's own shares, or by decreasing nominal or accounting value of the shares. The company's creditors may seek adequate collaterals for their receivables from the company in case of a decrease in its basic capital and the procedure for decrease of the share capital is different when conducted in accordance with the provisions on protection of creditors.

As in the case of limited liability companies, contributions to the registered basic capital of a joint-stock company can be both in cash or in-kind. In general, in-kind contributions may be valued either by the company's shareholders (i.e., their consensus is needed) or by an expert valuator pursuant to a procedure prescribed by the Company Law. However, in the case of public joint-stock companies, an expert evaluator in the relevant procedure must always value in-kind contributions. Also, preference shares may not be issued against in-kind contributions to the basic capital of the company.

(c) Corporate Governance

As in the case of limited liability companies, joint-stock companies must have either a one-tier or two-tier corporate governance structure.

If a joint-stock company has a one-tier corporate governance structure, the bodies of such companies are the general assembly and one or more directors (if there are three or more directors, a board of directors is formed). If a joint-stock company has a two-tier corporate governance structure, the bodies of the joint-stock company are the general assembly, supervisory board, and one or more executive directors (again, if there are three or more executive directors, the executive board is formed).

Public joint-stock companies must have a board of directors (in the case of the one-tier corporate governance structure) or an executive board (in the case of a two-tier corporate governance structure), as they must have at least three directors or executive directors, depending on their respective corporate governance structure.

Joint-stock companies may also appoint a company secretary, in which case the company's articles of association must envisage this function. In addition, each joint-stock company is free as to how it will organize and apply the internal supervision/audit. However, each public joint-stock company must employ at least one person to be in charge of internal supervision/audit; this person must have certain qualifications prescribed by law (e.g., must have passed an audit exam, have at least three years of experience in audit, high degree of education and similar).

(d) Shareholders' Pre-Emption Rights

In general, each shareholder has a pre-emptive right to subscribe to newly issued shares. Such right is exercisable in proportion to the number of paid-in shares of the same class of shares held by such shareholders at the time of the adoption of the decision on the subscription of newly issued shares. The company's articles of association determine the procedure for the exercise of this right and the company is obliged to inform each shareholder who has a pre-emptive right about any decision to issue shares. The company is also obliged to ensure that the deadline for the execution of the pre-emptive right is at least thirty days from the date of the sending of the notification about the decision on issuance of shares. Such notification, *inter alia*, should contain the number of issued shares, their price, and the deadline for the use of the pre-emptive right.

(e) Reporting Requirements

As to the reporting requirements, the level of such requirements depends on the type of the company. Namely, limited liability companies are obliged to register, once a year, financial reports and any change in the capital of the company that occurred in the preceding business year. In addition, each public joint-stock company is subject to certain reporting requirements, irrespective of whether its shares are traded on the regulated market or MTP/OTP, although such requirements are stricter if the shares are traded on the regulated market. The following paragraphs contain an overview of the main reporting requirements for public joint-stock companies:

(i) Annual Reports

A public joint-stock company is obliged to prepare an annual report, publish it (for the general public) and file it with the SEC. In addition, the company in question must submit each annual report to the regulated market or MTP/OTP if the securities of such company are traded in one of these markets within four months of the end of each financial year, as well as ensure that each such report is available to the general public for the minimum period of five years following the date of its publication.

An annual report includes:

- annual financial reports, together with the auditor's report;
- the company's annual business report;

- a statement by the persons responsible for the preparation of the annual report that, to the best of their knowledge, the annual financial report is prepared in accordance with the relevant international financial reporting standards (IFRS) and provides accurate and objective information about the assets, liabilities, financial position and performance, profits and losses, cash flows and changes in the capital of the company in question and of those its subsidiaries that are included in the consolidated reports.

An annual business report contains the following main information:

- an accurate presentation of the company's development and performance and, in particular, the company's financial position, as well as the information necessary for a proper valuation of the company's assets;
- a description of the company's expected future development, policy changes, and major risks and threats the company is facing;
- significant business events that occurred after the end of the financial year for which the report is being made;
- major transactions with related parties; and
- the company's research and development activities.

In the event that the relevant management body (typically the general assembly) of the company fails to adopt the annual report within four months of the end of the relevant financial year, the company is still obliged to publish the report by the end of the same period, including a remark that the report has not been adopted by the relevant management body. In such case, the company is obliged to inform the public, within seven days of the day on which the related decision is passed, that the report was eventually adopted by the relevant body of the company, as well as to publish the report once again in the event that it contains any changes in comparison to the previously published report.

The company is also obliged to publish the decision by the relevant management body on the adoption of the annual report and the decision on the distribution of profits or covering of losses unless such decisions represent an integral part of the annual report.

In addition to the above annual report, a company whose securities are admitted to trading on a regulated market/MTP is also obliged to produce and publish at least once a year an annual document that contains or refers to all information that was published or made available to the public over the preceding twelve months, in compliance with its obligations under the relevant rules.

The above annual document containing or referring to published information must be filed with the SEC not later than twenty business days after the publication of the company's annual audited financial statements and made available to the public in the manner prescribed by the relevant rules. In the event that such document makes a reference to certain information not contained therein, it should state where such information can be obtained and indicate which information is out-of-date (if any).

Also, companies of public interest, which are defined as such by the Law on Audit, are obliged to contemplate a yearly report on business activities as well as a corporate governance report, pursuant to the provisions of the Accounting Law. The companies of public interest are either joint-stock companies or limited liability companies which are considered to be large enterprises pursuant to the applicable accounting regulation, as well as public joint-stock companies, regardless of their size.

(ii) Semi-Annual Reports

A public joint-stock company, the securities of which are traded on a regulated market, is obliged to prepare its semi-annual report for the first six months of the respective financial year not later than two months from the end of the aforementioned six-month period. The report is prepared in accordance with the rules that apply to the preparation of annual reports. The semi-annual report must be published, as well as filed with the SEC and the regulated market on which the company's securities are traded.

Each semi-annual report must include the following main information:

- an abridged balance sheet, including a comparative overview of the information from the previous year's balance sheet;
- an abridged income statement, including a comparative overview of the information for the same period of the previous year;
- an abridged report on equity flows, including comparative information for the previous year;
- an abridged cash-flow statement, including comparative information for the same period of the previous year;
- accompanying notes, which must include adequate information to allow the comparison of the semi-annual report with the annual report, as well as adequate information and clarifications necessary for investors' proper understanding of all significant changes in relation to the amounts and events that have influenced the balance sheet and the income statement;
- the company's semi-annual business report, which must include a description of all significant events that occurred in the first six months of the financial year, the impact of such

events on the semi-annual report (including a description of risks and uncertainties for the remaining six months of the financial year), information on significant transactions with related parties executed in the first six months of the current financial year that have had a significant impact on the company's financial position and performance during that period, and any change in the transactions with related parties specified in the last annual report that could significantly influence the company's financial position or performance in the first six months of the current financial year;

- a statement from the persons responsible for the preparation of the semi-annual report that, to the best of their knowledge, the semi-annual financial report has been prepared in accordance with the relevant IFRS and provides accurate and objective information about the assets, liabilities, profits and losses, financial position and business operations of the company in question, including those subsidiaries that are included in the consolidated reports.

(iii) Quarterly Reports
A public joint-stock company whose securities are traded on the 'listing market' of the regulated market is obliged to prepare a quarterly report, publish it and file it with the SEC and the relevant regulated market within forty-five days of the end of each of the first three-quarters of the current financial year. The company must also ensure that the report is made available to the public for a minimum period of five years from the date of its publication.

(iv) Additional Information
A public joint-stock company is obliged to disclose promptly to the SEC and regulated market/MTP on which its shares and certain other similar securities are traded any change that occurs in the rights pertaining to such shares and other similar securities for each of their respective classes separately. A public company that is the issuer of securities which do not qualify as the aforementioned securities but which are traded on the regulated market/MTP is obliged to disclose promptly to the SEC and the regulated market/MTP any change in the rights arising from such securities, including any change in conditions that could indirectly influence the change in the rights attached to such securities and particularly any change pertaining to the loan terms and the interest rate.

(v) Reporting Duties Related to the Acquiring of a Company's Own Listed Shares
In the event that a public company acquires or sells its own voting shares, either independently or through a person acting in its name and on behalf of such company, the company is obliged to disclose promptly to the public the number of such shares both in

the absolute and relative amount and no later than within four trading days of the date of the acquisition or sale of the voting shares.

(vi) Other Reporting Duties of Public Companies Issuing Equity Securities

A public company that is the issuer of equity securities traded on the regulated market/MTP is obliged to, *inter alia*, ensure the availability of all the terms and information necessary for the company's shareholders to exercise their rights.

The public company is in particular obliged to:

- provide information about the place, time and agenda of the general assembly meeting, the total number of shares and the voting shares, and the shareholders' right to participate in the general assembly meeting in compliance with the company legislation;
- furnish any proxy statement in writing, electronically or otherwise, together with the announcement of the general assembly meeting, to any party with the right to vote in the general assembly meeting or, at the request of such party, also after the announcement of the general assembly meeting is issued;
- appoint a bank through which it will fulfil its financial obligations towards the shareholders;
- announce or issue a notification of the allocation and disbursement of dividends, as well as of the issuance of new shares, including the information about any prospective new allocation, subscription, cancellation or substitution.

A public company may also submit information to the shareholders electronically if that is approved at the general assembly meeting and if certain specific conditions are fulfilled.

A public company is under the obligation to submit promptly a proposal for any amendments to the articles of association to the SEC and the regulated market/MTP on which its shares are traded and no later than on the date of the publication of the announcement of the call for the relevant general assembly meeting on which such amendments are to be discussed/decided.

(vii) Reporting Duties Related to Insider Information

Issuers or persons acting on their behalf or for their account are obliged to compile a list of persons working for them through an employment relationship or otherwise who have access, on a regular basis or occasionally, to insider information relating, directly or indirectly, to the issuer. Lists of insiders must be regularly and promptly updated, submitted to the SEC upon its request, and kept by the company in question for at least five years following the moment they were initially compiled.

(viii) Language of Published Information

The general rule is that all the relevant information described above is published primarily in the Serbian language. However, a public company that is a foreign issuer and whose securities are traded on the regulated market/MTP in Serbia may publish the required information in another language in addition to Serbian.

(ix) Liability for Accuracy and Completeness of Published Information

Each issuer is considered legally liable for the accuracy and completeness of information that it submits to the SEC and the market operator and/or the regulated market and disclosed in accordance with the rules described above in the event that such information (including the prospectus or any of the information required to accompany the prospectus or the prospectus summary) contains materially false, inaccurate, or misleading information, or omits material facts that are necessary to prevent such information from being misleading. In addition to the issuer, the following persons are also considered legally liable:

- directors and members of the board of directors of the issuer unless the director has specifically voted against the authorization of the public offering;
- any person making an offer who is not an issuer;
- any guarantor of securities;
- the issuer's independent auditors, but only with respect to the audited financial statements included in or accompanying the prospectus that are covered by their audit report; and
- any other person upon whose authority or expertise a statement is included in the prospectus, but only with respect to the adequacy and accuracy of such statement.

In addition to the above persons, an investment firm providing underwriting services or serving as an agent in connection with the public offering is also deemed liable in the event that the prospectus or summary prospectus contains materially false, inaccurate or misleading information or omits material facts.

The SEC is not responsible for the authenticity and completeness of the information that has been submitted by issuers.

(x) Information Provided to Shareholders in Relation to General Assembly Meetings

The general rule is that the written notice of a regular general assembly meeting is given to each shareholder no less than thirty days before the date of such meeting. Similarly, written notice of an extraordinary general assembly meeting is given to each shareholder no less than twenty-one days before the date of such meeting. However, such deadlines may be shorter in some specific cases, or even assembly meetings may be held without notice, e.g., if all shareholders participate at a shareholders meeting of a non-public joint-stock company, and no one objects, then no prior notice for an assembly is required.

For each regular general assembly meeting, the company's board of directors or executive board must provide the shareholders with the following documents and information:

- financial reports (with related auditors' report, if the audit of financial reports is required by the relevant law);
- a proposed decision on profit distribution, if profit has been achieved;
- the text of any proposed decision, together with its rationale;
- the text of any contract or other legal transaction that is proposed for approval;
- a detailed description of any question proposed for debate, with comments or the opinion of the relevant body of the company (e.g., the board of directors);
- the annual and consolidated annual business reports;
- the supervisory board's report on the company's business operations and report on its supervision of the executive board (in case the company has a two-tier corporate governance structure); and
- any other document or information for which the company's board of directors or executive and supervisory board (in case the company has the two-tier corporate governance structure) consider to be of importance for the work and decision-making process of the company's general assembly.

Shareholders may also have access to other documents and information in the event that the board of directors or executive board deems that they are important for the operation and decision-making process of the general assembly.

The aforementioned information must be made available to the shareholders at the same time as the written notice of a regular general assembly meeting is given to them, either at the seat of the company, where shareholders themselves or their representatives may examine such information in person or on the website of the company, from where it can be downloaded completely. The notice of a general assembly meeting should contain information on the manner in which the information mentioned above may be accessed.

The company may envisage and outline additional means of disclosing such information in its articles of association.

2.1.4 Executive Authorities Within Serbian Companies

[41] Normally, authorized representatives of companies such as directors or members of the board of directors are empowered to exercise executive authority. Such persons are appointed either through the relevant reference in the foundation act of a company or the relevant decision of the company's general assembly. In addition to these persons, other persons can be elected through the relevant company's decisions to be authorized representatives of the company in question, e.g., other representatives, which are also registered in the Companies' Registry.

[42] Furthermore, a power of attorney may be issued by the company's general manager to the lawyers and/or other persons to act in certain matters in the name and on behalf of the company. In addition to this, the Company Law also provides for an institute of procuration, which represents a type of power of attorney which allows the procurators to conclude a large number of legal and/or other actions (except those for which it is required to have a special power of attorney such as the conclusion of loan agreements and/or representing company in litigation/ arbitration proceedings) in the name and on behalf of the company issuing procuration.

Procuration may be issued as an individual or a joint procuration, whereas, if nothing is specified, an issuance of individual procuration will be presumed. In the case of limited liability companies as well as joint-stock companies, the procuration is given by the general assembly of the relevant company, and it must be registered in the Companies' Register.

In addition, the so-called attorneys-in-fact by virtue of employment may represent a company. Those are persons who are, as employees of a company or by holding a business function within a company, regularly involved in entering into certain agreements or undertaking other actions on behalf of a company within the limits of their respective position and without a special power of attorney.

2.2 Laws Affecting M&A

[43] The main laws and regulations covering M&A activities in Serbia are the Company Law and the Takeover Law. Please note that the Takeover Law regulates mandatory takeovers (i.e., where a shareholder has passed certain thresholds of share ownership and must make a bid for the rest of the company's shares) and voluntary takeovers. The Takeover Law applies to takeovers of joint-stock companies with their seat in Serbia. However, based on the relevant criteria, certain joint-stock companies may be excluded from the scope of application of the Takeover Law (*see* paragraphs **[92]–[116]** below for more information on this issue). The Company Law provides for general corporate law rules that are relevant in the context of both public and private deals.

[44] Since the time of the last world economic crisis, the majority of M&A deals in Serbia have been private deals. Thus, takeovers of public companies have been relatively seldom, and such takeovers when they take place are rarely hostile. All in all, at present, the majority of M&A deals in Serbia take place in the context of limited liability companies which makes them, by the nature of the relevant process, private. Also, in many situations, M&A deals have the form of indirect changes of ownership in the relevant Serbian entity as the shareholder structure in Serbia remains unchanged while the ownership changes hands at the level of holding companies that are incorporated somewhere abroad.

[45] In the context of takeover framework, the applicable rules do not provide for any difference between hostile and friendly takeovers. Namely, irrespective of whether the takeover is friendly or hostile, from the moment of publication of the notification of takeover intent until the completion of the takeover bid process, the target's company board of directors may not: (i) increase the target company's share capital; (ii) cause the target company to undertake extraordinary actions or enter into an agreement that would alter significantly the status of the target company's property or liabilities; or (iii) cause the target company to buy or sell treasury shares; and/or (iv) publish a takeover bid for another company, without the prior consent of the target company's general assembly which may decide on such issues with the simple majority of votes. Also, within the same period of time, the target company must not amend its articles of association so as to limit the number of votes carried by its voting shares. However, in the event such limitations already exist in the articles of association, the target company's general assembly can abolish such provisions with a simple majority of votes.

2.2.1 General Framework

[46] At least, in theory, the applicable legal framework in Serbia provides for a relatively flexible environment for company mergers and de-mergers. However, as a general matter, transformation of a company is not possible during the course of liquidation, except such transformation is a measure of the reorganization of the company in question.

[47] However, as a general matter, the practice of such company transformations is not very developed in Serbia and the applicable rules contain some unclear provisions. Consequently, one is quite likely to face practical challenges when trying to execute complex corporate changes.

[48] The following types of corporate transformations are possible in Serbia:

(1) so-called status changes (mergers, de-mergers and spin-offs); and
(2) change of a company's legal form:
  (i) Status Changes:
    (a) Merger by Acquisition (*Pripajanje*)
    A merger by acquisition is a merger in the course of which one or more companies (i.e., the so-called acquired company) cease to exist without being formally liquidated and are simultaneously transferred to an already-existing company (i.e., the so-called acquiring company) by means of transfer of all of their assets and liabilities in exchange for the issuance of shares/ownership interests in the acquiring company to the shareholders or members, as the case may be, of the acquired company.
    (b) Merger by Incorporation of a New Company (*Spajanje*)

A merger by incorporation of a new company is a merger in the course of which two or more companies (i.e., the companies to be terminated as a result of such merger) cease to exist without being formally liquidated while all their assets and liabilities are transferred to a newly founded company simultaneously with and in exchange for the issuance of shares/ownership interests of the newly founded company to the shareholders or members, as the case may be, of the companies terminated by such merger.

(c) De-Merger by Acquisition (*Podela uz pripajanje*)
In the context of de-mergers, a company that is to be terminated by de-merger ceases to exist without being formally liquidated and simultaneously transfers to two or more already-existing acquiring companies (i.e., de-merger by acquisition), or two or more newly formed companies (i.e., de-merger by incorporation), or a combination of the one or more existing and one or more newly formed companies all its assets and liabilities in exchange for the issuance to its shareholders/members of shares/ownership interests, as applicable, in the acquiring companies.

(d) Spin-Off
In this context, like in the case of de-mergers, the applicable framework in Serbia envisages three spin-off types. Namely, the company that decides to spin-off part of its operations does so by transferring the relevant assets and liabilities to one or more newly formed entities (i.e., spin-off by incorporation), or one or more existing companies (i.e., spin-off by acquisition), or a combination of one or more newly formed companies and one or more existing companies.

(e) Certain Common Features of Mergers, De-Mergers and Spin-Offs
The following are some of the features and formalities that need to be fulfilled that are shared by all of the above types of status changes:

- preparation of relevant financial statements (which, in most of the cases, need to be audited);
- preparation and execution of the contract regulating the relevant status change type (e.g., a merger contract);
- preparation of other relevant documents by the corporate bodies of the companies involved and relevant experts (if applicable), such as the board of directors, auditors' and supervisory boards' reports;
- filing of the relevant documents (e.g., corporate resolutions, merger contract) with the Companies' Register;
- making available relevant documents regarding the planned status change at the registered seats of the merging companies for inspection by the shareholders and providing free copies thereof to such parties;

- publication of the contract regulating the transformation on the website of the company (if such website exists) and on the website of the Companies' Register not later than sixty days before the date on which the general assembly meeting is supposed to be held to take the decision on the prospective status change;
- approval of the status change by the general assemblies of the companies involved; and
- registration of the status change in the Companies' Register.

(ii) An additional common feature for all status changes is that, if so determined as part of the agreed process, shareholders receiving shares/ownership interests in the companies 'surviving' the relevant status change can also receive a cash payment, which may not exceed 10% of the nominal or accounting value of the shares/ownership interests issued in the relevant process.

(iii) Change of a Legal Form
Under Serbian law, it is possible to transform a company's current legal form into another one. The company with the new legal form is the legal successor of the entity that existed prior to such transformation taking place. Consequently, any licenses that are not dependent on the company's legal form remain in place. The change of the legal form of a company requires registration in the Companies' Register and the relevant procedure and formalities on the form the company had before transformation and the company type in which it is transformed.

As a general matter, there is an increasing trend to transform joint-stock companies into limited liability companies, which are less regulated and have completely relaxed capital requirements.

[49] Although the general corporate governance culture is not so developed in Serbia and the majority of Serbian companies are limited liability companies, there are a number of companies that are adopting and implementing internal regulations such as code of corporate governance, code of ethics, rulebooks on certain important business matters and similar. These voluntary codes and self-regulations represent so-called soft law and there are no formal fines in case companies fail to comply with them. However, the level of implementation of such internal regulations may show how far the relevant Serbian company has gone in the process of development of its corporate governance culture.

2.3 Relevant Regulatory Authorities

[50] The current Serbian Government comprises twenty-five ministries, each responsible for overseeing activities in their respective fields (e.g., defence, justice, health) in addition to three ministers who act without a portfolio (*ministar bez portfelja*). Those ministries are, through the Government, the main proponents of laws in their fields of competence and the main interpreters of such laws.

[51] Additionally, there are over one hundred different specialized governmental agencies exercising substantial authority in their own respective areas (e.g., Energy Agency, Agency for Energy Efficiency, Regulatory Agency for Electronic Communications and Postal Services). Having such a large number of regulators with broad competencies (which overlap to a certain degree in some instances) has resulted in conflicting interpretations of the same laws on the one hand and a legal vacuum in other cases. This situation is often publicly criticized and it appears that there are plans to decrease the number of regulators and clearly divide their authorities.

2.4 Key Market Regulators

2.4.1 Main Regulatory Bodies in Charge of Foreign Investments and Trade

[52] The bodies in charge of foreign investments comprise in the most general sense, *inter alia*, the Ministry of Internal and External Trade, Information and Telecommunications, Ministry of Commerce, Council of Economic Development and RAS.

[53] In the area of foreign economic relations, the Ministry of Internal and External Trade has an important role as it is responsible for creating, implementing, proposing and improving the regimes governing foreign trade. Also, this ministry has competencies in relation to the trade in goods, services and industrial property rights, as well as foreign trade and the system of export-import control of arms, military equipment and other controlled goods. In addition, it concludes and monitors the application of international trade contracts and agreements and proposes and adopts, as appropriate, regulations in the area of foreign investments, concessions, and public-private partnerships.

[54] The Ministry of Commerce is, *inter alia*, responsible for: proposing measures to encourage investments, coordinating activities related to investments, and coordinating public agencies responsible for the promotion of exports and investment (such as RAS).

[55] The Council of Economic Development monitors the situation in the field of regional development, proposes measures for the promotion of such development, advances the goals of regional development and encourages their implementation. RAS' role is to, among other things, focus on the administration of various incentives offered by the relevant framework in Serbia. For more information on these and other issues, *see* paragraphs **[72]–[89]** below.

[56] In the below paragraphs, we provide a summary overview of the main regulatory bodies and their respective competencies in the area of capital markets and competition.

2.4.2 Capital Markets

[57] The main regulator of Serbia's capital markets is the SEC, which has numerous responsibilities under the Capital Markets Law, Takeover Law, Law on Alternative Investment Funds and Law on Open Investment Funds Subject to the Public Offer. In this respect, it is worth mentioning that the SEC enacted a series of by-laws in 2022 on the basis of the newly introduced Capital Markets Law in order to comply with the new regulatory framework governing investment funds and other relevant matters. SEC's main responsibilities include: approving public offerings and admission to trading of financial instruments; granting licenses to investment firms, market operators and fund operators; approving the acquisition of a 'qualified participation'; approving of the appointment of directors in the market operator, investment firms and the Central Register; monitoring the activities of issuers and public companies; and general compliance with the laws that fall within its jurisdiction.

2.4.3 Competition

[58] The authority in charge of supervision of the implementation of the competition law framework in Serbia is the Competition Authority, whose main responsibilities include: merger control; sanctioning of monopolistic and other anticompetitive behaviours and arrangements; monitoring and analysis of competition conditions on particular markets and particular sectors; and undertaking activities aimed at developing awareness on the need for protection of competition. For more information on Merger Controls and Antitrust/Competition Issues, *see* paragraphs **[156]–[184]** below.

2.4.4 Obtaining Governmental Approvals

[59] Serbian regulatory authorities are generally bound by and operate pursuant to the rules and procedural deadlines prescribed by the Administrative Proceedings Law, which oblige them to issue legal acts, including various decisions, conclusions and legal opinions, as soon as possible but in any event within thirty days (or sixty days in more complex cases). There are, of course, some exceptions to this general dynamic, and these need to be assessed on a case-by-case basis.

[60] Persons who submit the request for such acts may try to expedite the process by submitting the so-called urgency letters to the competent bodies. It is also important to note that the applicable deadlines for issuance of relevant legal acts are typically calculated from the moment the relevant private party submits the complete set of necessary documents. In practice, this means that the actual period of time within which the relevant body processes a request is often longer because the applicants are asked to amend, supplement or otherwise change the initial application with the view of avoiding its rejection.

[61] An appeals process is generally available in case of both rejection of a party's request and failure by the competent body to issue the relevant ruling. Similarly, a further judicial review of the proceedings and administrative acts is also available in most cases.

[62] A party in proceedings before the regulatory bodies may be any natural or legal person (including state authorities, organizations and other entities), but engaging a professional advisor/representative, such as lawyers, is highly recommended.

[63] Administrative fees do not differ in the event the private party involved in administrative proceedings is a foreign investor. A foreign investor should, however, expect additional costs related to actions such as certification and translation of any documents obtained outside Serbia.

2.5 Controls/Restrictions on Foreign Investment

[64] In Serbia, a foreign investor may incorporate or invest in a company engaging in almost any kind of business activity without any limitation. Also, there are no minimum capital requirements imposed specifically in respect of foreign-owned companies, and foreign-owned companies are not required to obtain any specific permit to trade. However, they will need to (under the same terms as purely domestic companies) obtain certain approvals/permits in some specific cases, such as the wholesaling of medicines and tobacco and the export and import of silver (unprocessed, raw, semi-manufactured, or as dust) and gold (unprocessed, semi-manufactured, or as dust).

[65] The main limitation on the ability of foreign natural and legal persons to purchase real property in Serbia is the principle of 'reciprocity', whereby foreign natural and legal persons may purchase real property in Serbia, provided that Serbian citizens have an equal right to acquire and own real property in the respective foreign country. A further limitation on the ability of foreigners to acquire real property in Serbia is if such property is located in those parts of the country that are designated as zones in which foreign natural and legal persons may not acquire real property (typically in border areas). In addition, as already noted above, foreigners can acquire and own agricultural land in Serbia under certain conditions (*see* paragraph **[24]** above for more information on conditions for foreigners to acquire agricultural and in Serbia).

[66] Additionally, the applicable framework in Serbia imposes certain restrictions on foreign investments in some sectors. The following is an overview of the main such restrictions.

2.5.1 Banking

[67] Obtaining a licence from the NBS is a general precondition for establishing a bank in Serbia irrespective of the nationality of its founders. However, issuing a license to a foreign bank or financial institution to establish a bank in Serbia is conditional upon providing to the NBS, *inter alia*, a proof that the regulatory body of the applicant's home country undertakes supervision on a consolidated basis (i.e., over the combined financial statements of the relevant parent company and its subsidiaries) in a manner that meets the conditions prescribed by the NBS, as well as that there is adequate cooperation between the NBS and the regulatory body of the applicant's home country (i.e., a country in which the applicant is founded and received the relevant licence). Similarly, acquisition of qualifying ownership in a bank (i.e., ownership exceeding 5% of shares) is subject to the prior approval of the NBS, which approval is obtained in a very elaborate procedure in which the NBS assesses whether the prospective acquirer meets all the relevant conditions.

2.5.2 Utilities

[68] Certain utility services, such as the supply of drinking water and public transportation, may exclusively be performed by public utility companies founded by local municipalities, limited liability companies and joint-stock companies whose sole owner is a public company or local municipality as well as a subsidiary of such entities. However, it is possible that a public entity delegates the performance of certain tasks within the aforementioned activities to private entities.

2.5.3 Energy

[69] Energy activities are designated as activities of the so-called public interest, such as transport and operation of a natural gas transmission network, transport of electricity and operation of an electricity transmission network, distribution of electricity and operation of the related distribution network, as well as distribution and supply of heat. Such activities may be performed by foreign companies only pursuant to an agreement concluded with the state, an autonomous province, or the relevant local municipality.

2.5.4 Mining

[70] The Mining Law declares that branches of foreign entities registered in Serbia are entitled to perform geological explorations/exploitation if they fulfil conditions prescribed by 'the law that regulates the rights of foreign persons in relation to the use of assets of public interest'. However, in line with the law governing concessions, a foreign entity may be granted a concession for the purpose of exploration and/or exploitation of mineral resources. This appears to potentially imply that a foreign investor would need to obtain a concession right for the purpose of exploiting the relevant resource.

In light of the foregoing, it appears that direct involvement of a foreign company in the context of geological explorations and, especially, exploitation would be potentially impractical in light of the possibility that this would trigger a need to organize a concession process. Accordingly, it is advisable that, instead, foreign investors form or acquire Serbian entities for the purpose of developing mining projects.

[71] However, the export and import of silver (unprocessed, raw, semi-manufactured, or as dust) and gold (unprocessed, semi-manufactured, or as dust) are subject to prior approval by the relevant ministry. Further, uranium and thorium alloys and compounds and other elements identified as sources of ionizing radiation may only be imported or exported with the permission of the competent authority.

2.6 Incentives for Foreign Investment

2.6.1 FDI Framework

[72] The main rules on guarantees and safeguards for investors in Serbia are outlined in the Investment Law, according to which foreign and domestic investments are treated equally. According to the Investment Law, the following is considered to constitute an investment: (i) direct investment, i.e., investment in material and non-material assets of a company; and (ii) indirect investment, i.e., acquiring an ownership interest or shares in the capital of a company.

[73] Serbia has developed a range of incentives and safeguards designed to attract FDIs, including tax incentives in the form of tax credits and reduced corporate tax rates. The Serbian Government established a specially designated organization, the RAS, for the purpose of, *inter alia*, assisting FDI in Serbia and administering the relevant incentive package.

[74] The main investment incentives and safeguards that are currently in force as well as other relevant foreign investment principles/safeguards are summarized in the sections below.

2.6.2 General Incentives

[75] A special decree on incentives for direct investments provides for, *inter alia*, a number of state grants that depend on the size of the investment project and on the level of development of the area where new jobs will be created. Investment projects for which funds can be allocated range from an investment whose total value is greater than ranges prescribed by the decree, e.g., EUR500 000 and which creates at least fifty new jobs in the region of the capital of Serbia, (ii) EUR400 000 and which creates at least forty new jobs for indefinite period of time in the Vojvodina region, and (iii) EUR300 000 and which creates at least thirty new jobs for indefinite period of time in the so-called devastated areas of Serbia. For investment in service centres for cross-border services provided through different means of communications, eligible projects are those with a value greater than EUR150 000 and which create at least fifteen new jobs for an indefinite period of time. The investors in devastated areas may be granted funds in the amount of up to 30% of the eligible costs of two-year gross salaries or a maximum of EUR5 000 per new job created. In the most developed areas of Serbia, the amount of state grants can reach up to 25% of the eligible costs of two-year gross salaries or a maximum of

EUR3 000 per new job created. For labour-intensive projects, where more than 100 new jobs are created, the amount of funds shall be increased by a further 10%, or by even 15%, where more than 200 jobs are created, i.e., by 20%, where more than 500 jobs are created. Upon receiving the state grants, the beneficiaries must not reduce their headcount over a period of five years for large enterprises and three years for small and medium enterprises. Please note that the acquisition of shares in a company shall not be considered to constitute direct investment within the purpose and meaning of the aforementioned decree.

[76] The state funds for attracting direct investment may be used for financing investment projects in the manufacturing sector and for the service centre businesses. However, the funds may not be used for financing investment projects in the traffic sector, software development (unless the software is developed for the purpose of improvement of a product, production process or the service of service centres), the hospitality industry, lottery, retail, the production of synthetic fibres, coal and steel, tobacco and tobacco products, arms and munitions, shipbuilding, airports, utility sector, energy sector, broadband networks, fishing and aquaculture.

2.6.3 Tax Incentives

[77]

(i) Corporate Profit Tax Holiday.
Companies are eligible for corporate profit tax exemption for a period of up to ten years starting from the first year in which they report taxable profit if they invest in fixed assets whose value exceeds RSD1 bn (approximately EUR8.5 m), provided that throughout the investment period, they employ at least one hundred additional employees.

(ii) Carrying Forward of Losses.
The tax loss from the business, financial or non-business transactions stated in the tax return can be carried forward and offset against future profits over a period of up to five years.

(iii) Avoiding Double Taxation.
If a taxpayer has already paid tax on profit generated abroad, he is entitled to a corporate profit tax credit in Serbia. The same right is enjoyed by a resident taxpayer who earns revenue and pays personal income tax in another country, provided there is a double taxation treaty with that country. Serbia signed sixty double taxation treaties with other countries, including Austria, The Netherlands, Germany, Cyprus and the Russian Federation.

2.6.4 Other Direct/Indirect Incentives

[78]

(i) Customs-Free Imports of Raw Materials and Semi-Finished Goods.
Foreign investors in Serbia can enjoy the benefit of customs-free import of raw materials and semi-finished goods for export-oriented production. This

benefit can either be achieved by operating in one of the free zones in Serbia or by a permit from the customs office for outward processing production. In both cases, finished products must be 100% designated for export.

(ii) Customs-Free Imports of Machinery and Equipment.
Foreign investors are exempt from paying customs duty on imported equipment and machinery which represents the in-kind contribution of a foreign investor in the capital of a company in Serbia, except for import of passenger motor vehicles and slot and gambling machines.

2.6.5 Special Regime for Trade in Goods under International Treaties

[79] Serbia has concluded a number of treaties that enable the customs-free trade of goods that originate in Serbia.

[80] The Association and Stabilization Treaty stipulates, *inter alia*, that exports to the EU market are free of customs duty. Under this treaty, export quantities are limited by annual quotas for several food products (e.g., baby beef, sugar and wine).

[81] The free trade agreement that Serbia concluded with the Russian Federation stipulates that goods produced in Serbia having at least 51% value added in the country are considered to be of Serbian origin and are exported to the Russian Federation customs-free. The list of products that are excluded from the free trade agreement is revised annually and it currently includes items such as cars and tobacco.

[82] The agreement Serbia concluded with EFTA Member States (Switzerland, Norway, Iceland and Liechtenstein) stipulates that industrial products exported from Serbia into the EFTA Member States are exempted from customs duties, except for a very limited number of goods, including fish and other seafood products.

2.6.6 Free Zones

[83] Currently, in Serbia, there are fifteen industrial zones that are licensed free customs zones. They are: Pirot, Subotica, Zrenjanin, FAS Kragujevac, Šabac, Novi Sad, Užice, Smederevo, Svilajnac, Apatin, Kruševac, Vranje, Priboj, Belgrade and Šumadija Kragujevac.

[84] Import into and export from these zones are free of Value Added Tax (VAT) and customs duties, while income generated from production within such zones is exempt from taxation. Salaries and incomes generated within free zones can be transferred to any country, including Serbia, without a need for prior approval and free of taxes.

2.6.7 Guarantees Against Nationalization and Expropriation

[85] One of the main principles guaranteed to foreign investors by the Investment Law is legal certainty, meaning that the rights granted to a foreign investor at the moment of the incorporation of its entity in Serbia cannot be restricted by any subsequent amendments to the relevant laws and by-laws. The stake/capital contribution of a foreign investor cannot be subject to expropriation and similar state measures, except in cases of public interest (as determined by law) and with compensation comprising the market value of the object of expropriation prior to announcing intent for expropriation and compensation for decrease in value in business caused by such expropriation.

2.6.8 Guarantee for Repatriation of Profits

[86] As a general matter, foreign investors are guaranteed the right to transfer abroad their profits realized in Serbia. This right is subject to the obligation to pay all applicable taxes in Serbia.

[87] Various formal and technical aspects for payments, collections and transfers between residents and non-residents are generally regulated by the Foreign Exchange Law. Under this law, a general rule is that payments, collections and transfers made in the course of transactions between residents and non-residents are executed freely, without restrictions. However, some restrictions may apply especially in the context of transfer/assignment of receivables and debt between resident and non-resident, as well as in case of delayed payments of goods and services in excess of one year since the date when goods and services are imported. Also, loans granted by foreign residents (e.g., banks) to Serbian residents must be notified to the NBS.

2.6.9 Ownership of Immovable Property by Foreigners

[88] In Serbia, foreign natural and legal persons may acquire immovable property under certain limitations. The main limitation is the principle of 'reciprocity', whereby foreign natural and legal persons may purchase real property in Serbia provided that it is determined that Serbian citizens have an equal right to acquire and own real property in the respective foreign country(ies). Further limitations on the ability of foreigners to acquire real property in Serbia are if such property is located in those parts of the country that are designated as zones in which foreign natural and legal persons may not acquire real property or in case of agricultural land.

[89] Subject to the limitations set forth above: (i) foreign natural and legal persons that execute business activities in Serbia may acquire real property that is necessary for the conduct of such business activities; and (ii) foreign natural persons that do not conduct business activities in Serbia may acquire apartments and residential buildings in the country. Furthermore, the inheriting of real property in Serbia by foreign natural persons is allowed, again subject to the reciprocity requirement, but, according to practice, reciprocity is assumed in the case of inheritance of real property. However, it is not clear if the other limitation (relating to so-called prohibited zones) would apply in such a case.

2.6.10 Off-Shore Bank Accounts

[90] According to the currently applicable rules, companies that are Serbian residents may hold foreign currency in bank accounts abroad only in certain specific cases and, typically, subject to the prior approval of the NBS. For example, this is possible when foreign currency is needed for the purposes of financing construction or exploration works abroad or making a guarantee deposit for the purpose of participating in a bidding or tender procedure in another country. When filing an application for permission to hold foreign currency in a bank account abroad, the company-Serbian resident is obliged to file all supporting documents needed as evidence of the purpose of holding foreign currency abroad.

2.6.11 Specific Issues of Company/Securities Law

[91]

(i) Shareholder Approval.
Although day-to-day management of companies is entrusted to the directors or board of directors/executive board, depending on the company form and specific corporate governance structure (*see* paragraphs **[39]–[40]** above for more information on this), shareholders have certain statutory competencies that interfere with the general monopoly of directors in relation to such day-to-day management and that are relevant in the context of M&A transactions.

For example, under the applicable Serbian rules, shareholders' approval is required for any transaction in the course of which the company in question disposes/acquires assets whose value is equal to or higher than 30% of the book/market value (as stated in the most recent annual balance sheet) of all the company's assets, regardless of the form of consideration. The shareholders' decision on approval must be adopted by at least three-fourths of the votes of shareholders present at the general assembly's meeting. If this rule is disobeyed, a shareholder who holds at least 5% of the shares of the company in question is entitled to request (within the period of six months since the general assembly's meeting at which the business report for the business year during which the transaction took place was reviewed, but not more than three years from the transaction in question) the competent court to void the relevant transaction, under the condition that such shareholder held 5% of the shares of the company at the moment when the transaction took place.

However, the Company Law envisages that a sale or purchase of an asset that is undertaken within the company's regular business activity does not fall within the above limitation. Therefore, company directors are enabled to pursue transactions which are clearly within the scope of 'regular business activities' without fear that they will be hindered or even blocked by the need to obtain shareholders' approval.

(ii) Directors' Duties.

The Company Law sets out the following duties of directors in respect of a company:

(a) duty to exercise his/her duties with diligence, the care of prudent businessmen, and in the reasonable belief that he/she is acting in the best interests of the company;

(b) duty to declare any personal interest in any proposed and existing transaction and to ask for the approval of such transaction by a competent corporate body;

(c) duty to avoid conflict of interest;

(d) duty to keep business secrets confidential;

(e) duty (after leaving the company in question) to respect the ban on engaging in activities that constitute competition with such company; and

(f) duty to act within his/her powers (i.e., a company's representatives are required to act in accordance with the limitations on their powers, as set out under law and in decisions made by the company bodies).

As to the duty to act within his/her powers, any limitations on directors' powers generally do not apply to third persons. The only exception to this rule applies in the case there is a co-signing obligation that is as such duly registered in the Companies' Register. Directors/other representatives of companies are liable for damage arising as a consequence of a breach of the aforementioned duties.

As mentioned above, directors have a duty of loyalty to their company. Hence, if a director breaches any of his/her duties, it is up to the company (i.e., shareholders, since they ultimately control the company) to decide whether the company will take action against such director (e.g., dismiss the director or file a claim against the director).

With the exception of takeovers, Serbian law is silent on the specific duties of directors of companies engaged in M&A toward shareholders, creditors, employees, or others. Thus, as a general matter, a director of a company engaged in an M&A transaction would have to comply with all the aforementioned (regular) duties envisaged by the Company Law. As for the specific obligations of company directors in the context of takeovers, *see* paragraphs **[43]–[45]** above for more information on this subject.

(iii) Financial Assistance.

Under the Company Law, the provision of financial assistance is prohibited, and this prohibition applies to limited liability companies and joint-stock companies alike. The Company Law prohibits a target company from extending financial assistance of any kind for the purposes of the acquisition of its shares/ownership interests, either directly or indirectly. In this regard, the Company Law expressly lists loans, guarantees, sureties and collateral as prohibited actions. The Company Law further stipulates that any legal transaction contrary to the financial assistance rules shall be null and void. There are very few precedents (if any) regarding this issue and the legislation does not provide for any 'whitewash procedures'.

(iv) Security Interests.
In principle, pledges over movable assets and mortgages over immovable assets are the two main types of security interests under Serbian law.

The Pledge Law recognizes, *inter alia*, the pledge of a 'movable generic item' (*stvar određena po vrsti*), such as the pledge over pledger's commodities held in a warehouse.

The amendments to the Pledge Law adopted in April 2019 introduce a more elaborate provision with respect to the possibility of pledging a group of assets and inventory. Namely, the Pledge Law now explicitly provides that a group of movable assets (including inventory) that is situated at a specific place and consists of movables that are intended for sale or lease, as well as raw materials and materials used to carry out a business activity, may be subject to a pledge. If certain movables become part of the group of movable assets following the registration of the pledge, the pledge shall extend to such newly acquired movables by operation of law, provided that such movables are owned by the pledger. This amendment seems to bring the concept of a group of movable assets and inventory closer to the 'floating charge' concept of common law (primarily in terms of the widening of the scope of assets it may encompass). However, note that the concept of a 'floating charge' over all assets is not recognized under Serbian law.

Pursuant to the amendments to the Pledge Law adopted in April 2019, it will be possible to register a right to a possessory pledge and retention of ownership right based on an agreement on the sale of movables that is aimed at securing the rights of the seller until the payment of the purchase price in total. Such a retention of ownership rights may have an impact on creditors of the purchaser, but only if the retention of ownership rights is registered in the Pledge Register prior to the purchaser's insolvency or seizure of its property.

Although the aforementioned concepts have been regulated by the Law on Contracts and Torts for decades, it has previously been impossible to register such rights in a public register. It remains to be seen whether the possibility of registering such rights will now make their use more appealing to market participants, as based on our experience, these concepts have not been frequently utilized in practice to date.

In addition, it is possible to establish a pledge of future items or rights (including receivables). However, the pledge may be registered over the future item or right, but it is not perfected until such right is acquired by the pledger. Once the pledger has acquired the item or right, the pledge is perfected and is enforceable, like any other registered pledge.

Pledges are generally perfected upon their registration in the relevant register.

The following are the main types of mortgages/pledges pursuant to Serbian law.

(v) Mortgages.
Depending on the manner in which they are established, there are three general types of mortgages: contractual mortgages, unilateral mortgages (*založna izjava*) and court mortgages. In principle, mortgages are established once they have been duly registered with the competent Real Estate Register.

Contractual and unilateral mortgages are currently the market standard in Serbia and they are relatively similar both in terms of form and content, as well as registration requirements. A contractual mortgage is concluded on the basis of a written contract entered into between the owner of the real property and the creditor. Such a mortgage agreement must stipulate the property over which the mortgage is being established and the secured receivable. The mortgage agreement must be notarized.

The same formal requirements apply to a unilateral mortgage. Namely, the relevant mortgage declaration is a document notarized by the competent notary public. As mentioned above, its content is practically the same as that of a mortgage agreement. A court mortgage is concluded before a judge in the form of a court-supervised settlement agreement. It must include all the relevant details of the mortgaged property and the underlying receivable. This type of mortgage is somewhat less frequent in practice nowadays.

The enforcement mechanism at the foreclosure stage may vary, depending on the type of mortgage. Namely, the so-called contractual and unilateral mortgages are typically designated by the party (or parties) as mortgages that can be enforced through an extrajudicial procedure, while the so-called court mortgage is enforced solely through a court-managed procedure. However, depending on the intention of the secured creditor, contractual and unilateral mortgages may also be enforced through a court-managed procedure. Each of the mortgage types has certain advantages and disadvantages and the decision as to which one should be used in each particular case typically depends on the circumstances (e.g., whether only one or more real properties need to be mortgaged at the same time, as well as their location):

(a) Pledges of Movables and Receivables.
Pledges are established on the basis of a written agreement entered into between the pledger and the pledgee. All pledged movables must be specified in the pledge agreement. However, as mentioned above, it is also possible to create a pledge on a movable generic item (*stvari određene po rodu*). A pledge of movable assets is perfected upon its registration with the Pledge Register. As with other pledges, a pledge of receivables is perfected upon its entry in the Pledge Register.

(b) Pledge of Ownership Interest
A pledge of an ownership interest in a limited liability company is based on a written pledge agreement, and signatures thereon should be certified. The pledging of ownership interests can be freely effected by the company's members unless otherwise provided by the company's foundation act. The pledge is perfected when it is registered in the Pledge Register. In the event of a default on the part of the pledger, formally speaking, the pledgee can enforce the pledge in any manner that it sees

fit (provided that it is in accordance with the Pledge Law), including, without limitation, by way of an extrajudicial sale through public auction.

(c) Pledge of Shares

Shareholders in a joint-stock company often secure loans provided to the joint-stock company in question (i.e., particularly if such joint-stock company is a subsidiary within a company group) by pledging the shares they hold in the joint-stock company to the lender. A pledge of shares is based on a written pledge agreement and is perfected upon its registration with the Central Register (and not the Pledge Register) pursuant to the authorization of the registered owner of such shares. The multiple pledging of shares is allowed.

The pledgee is not entitled to exercise the rights connected with any pledged shares (e.g., receive dividend payments) unless the pledge agreement provides otherwise. If the debt secured by the pledged shares is not settled fully and on time, the pledgee is entitled to sell the shares. The pledgee must inform the pledger of the intended sale before it takes place.

As a general matter, in the event of default and in case such right is defined in the pledge agreement, pledges can be enforced in an out-of-court procedure. In the case of extrajudicial enforcement, there are certain formalities to be followed (e.g., notification to the pledger about the intention to sell the pledged asset and registration of the commencement of the enforcement in the Pledge Register). The pledger may sell the pledge at its market/stock market value only if that possibility is envisaged under the pledge agreement.

However, if an insolvency proceeding has been opened against the company that serves as the pledger, then the general rules stipulated by the Insolvency Act apply. Pursuant to these rules, secured creditors (*razlučni poverioci*) may enforce their secured interest only within the insolvency proceeding. Consequently, any commenced enforcement proceedings are deemed to have been terminated by the opening of the insolvency proceedings.

As to the status of secured creditors in insolvency proceedings, some special rules apply whose purpose is to ensure that secured creditors collect their claim from the value of a particular asset/value of the company before any other creditor within the insolvency proceedings. Furthermore, the secured creditor may, in theory, ask to be exempted from the insolvency proceedings.

(vi) Completion Formalities.

Depending on the type of transaction and assets involved, completion formalities might be different. For example, completion formalities concerning the transfer of ownership interest are different in comparison to the completion formalities related to the transfer of real estate. The following is a brief overview of the relevant formalities in the case of the most common transaction types.

(vii) Completion Formalities Related to Transfer of Real Property.

In order to effect a transfer of ownership title over real estate, such as buildings or land, the parties (i.e., seller and purchaser) must conclude a written and notarized acquisition agreement before the competent notary public. However, the transfer of the ownership title is effective only once the purchaser has been registered as the owner of the property in the Real Estate Register. For the purpose of such registration, the notary performing the relevant notarization submits ex officio a request for registration along with the original acquisition agreement to the Real Estate Register (direct submission for registration by the contractual parties is still possible, although not practical). The Real Estate Register is obliged to process such request and register the ownership title of the purchaser, provided that all relevant conditions are met, within fifteen days of the submission of such request. However, this process might take considerably longer in case there are pending requests related to the same real property, or in case the Real Estate Register requires additional documents from the purchaser.

(viii) Completion Formalities Related to Transfer of Shares in Joint-Stock Companies.

Registration of the ownership title over shares is required in order for such transfer to be effective. The legal basis for the transfer is the acquisition of shares on capital markets or pursuant to an acquisition agreement (e.g., in the case of the acquisition of shares of privately held joint-stock companies). In the case of the latter, the parties' signatures on the relevant agreement must be certified.

(ix) Completion Formalities Related to Transfer of Ownership Interest in Limited Liability Companies.

In order for a transfer to be effective, in addition to a written agreement on transfer of the ownership agreement on which the parties' signatures have been certified, the registration of the transfer with the Companies' Register is also required.

Generally, the relevant state authority may require certain additional documents to be submitted/presented in the course of the execution of the relevant transaction/transfer. For example, during the process of the certification of the parties' signatures on the relevant acquisition agreement, the notary public may require to be presented with the respective extract from the companies' register of both the acquirer and seller. Furthermore, provided that the acquirer is a foreign company, the notarization and/or super legalization of relevant documents with an Apostille is required. In addition, the translation of any relevant document written in a foreign language by court-sworn translators is also required.

(x) Costs and Fees.

Transaction fees differ in terms of amount depending on the type of transaction.

As regards the notarization of an asset acquisition agreement (e.g., an agreement on purchase of real estate), the relevant fee will be calculated in relation to the value of the purchased asset. Such fees for transactions involving entities usually range between RSD45 000 (approximately EUR380) and the general notarial fee cap of RSD720 000 (approximately EUR6 100).

With regard to the certification of the parties' signatures on a share purchase/transfer agreement (agreement on purchase of ownership interest, agreement on purchase of shares), the relevant fee will be calculated in relation to the type of parties involved and the number of signatures with the certification of one signature of a company representative per document copy being approximately EUR10. Such fees usually range between RSD7 500 (approximately EUR65) and RSD18 900 (approximately EUR160).

Certain other administrative fees depend on the type of the transaction. For example, the administrative fee for the registration of the title over an ownership interest at the Companies' Register is RSD3 100 (approximately EUR30) plus RSD3 100 (approximately EUR30) for the registration of the new foundation act of the company. However, the administrative fee for the registration of ownership title over real property in the Real Estate Register is usually RSD5 550 (approximately EUR47).

Furthermore, the relevant fee for merger clearance charged by the Competition Authority is up to EUR25 000 (for phase I proceedings) or up to EUR50 000 (for phase II proceedings) depending on the type of proceeding in which this body is processing the relevant merger filing (*see* paragraphs **[156]–[184]** below for more information on merger filings). This is by far the highest administrative fee that is being charged in the context of transactions in Serbia.

One should also bear in mind that various notarization, certification and/or Apostille fees/costs regarding relevant documents may be incurred abroad in relation to a transaction taking place in Serbia if the acquirer/parties are foreign companies or natural persons. In addition, costs related to the translation of documents which are in a foreign language are also likely to be incurred and, at the moment, such costs typically range between EUR10–EUR15 per page of the English to Serbian language translation (costs may increase depending on the urgency and language).

(xi) Disclosure and Similar Notification Obligations in Relation to Transactions. As a general rule, public joint-stock companies are obliged to disclose promptly to the SEC and the regulated market/MTP on which its shares are traded any change that occurs in the rights pertaining to such shares (for each class of shares separately). Also, a public company that is the issuer of securities which are not shares but are traded on the regulated market/MTP is obliged to disclose promptly to the SEC and the regulated market/MTP any change in the rights arising from such securities, including any change in conditions that could indirectly influence the change in the rights attached to such securities and particularly any change pertaining to the loan terms and the interest rate.

Furthermore, a person (natural or legal) who/that directly or indirectly reaches, exceeds or falls under 5%, 10%, 15%, 20%, 25%, 30%, 50% and 75% of the voting rights in a joint-stock company whose shares are traded on a regulated market/MTP, is obliged to notify of such fact the company in question, SEC, and regulated market/MTP on which the shares of such company are traded. The aforementioned reporting obligation also applies in situations in which the number of voting shares or votes attached to such shares changes to the extent that one of the relevant thresholds is triggered. Please note that additional reporting thresholds may apply in the case of companies that operate in certain industries.

The person obliged to make the necessary notification is the person who/that holds the relevant voting shares or depository receipts either directly or indirectly and in his/her/its own name and on his/her/its own account or in his/her/its own name but on account of some other natural or legal person. In addition, the aforementioned notification obligation applies to a natural or legal person holding directly or indirectly financial instruments which, by means of a unilateral expression of intent or on the basis of a binding legal transaction, give him/her/it the right to acquire already issued voting shares in a public company, which are traded on the regulated market/MTP.

A public joint-stock company, the shares of which are traded on a regulated market/MTP and in which there has been a change in the number of voting shares, is obliged to make public, at the end of each calendar month, the changes that occurred and the revised total number of voting shares, as well as the nominal value of the company's registered basic capital.

The aforementioned notification obligation also applies to a person (legal or natural) who acquires, sells, holds or exercises a voting right in one or more of the following cases:

(a) the voting right belongs to a third party with whom such person has concluded an agreement obliging them to adopt a common long-term policy for the management of the company in question through the joint exercise of the voting rights that they hold;
(b) the voting right was transferred temporarily, pursuant to a contract and for consideration by such person to a third party for the purpose of exercising such rights, provided that such transaction is in accordance with the law;
(c) the voting right is transferred to another natural or legal person as collateral when the person controls that voting right and expresses his/her/its will in exercising such rights, provided that such transaction is in accordance with the law;
(d) the voting right arising from shares for which the usufruct has been established on behalf of a natural or legal person;
(e) the voting rights that are held or that can be exercised (in the manner prescribed in bullet points a to d above) by a company that is controlled by a natural or legal person;
(f) the voting rights from shares deposited with a natural or legal person, which such person may exercise independently, in whatever way that person decides at his own discretion, provided that there are no specific instructions from shareholders;
(g) the voting rights from shares held by a third party in his/her/its name and on the account of a natural or legal person; and
(h) the voting rights that such person may exercise as a proxy independently, in whatever manner that such person decides, provided that there are no specific instructions by shareholders.

The above notification must be submitted promptly but no later than by the expiry of four trading days, with the first trading day being the day after which the person who is obliged to make the aforementioned notification:

- becomes aware of the acquisition or the sale, or the possibility of exercising the voting rights or could have become aware of it, considering the circumstances, irrespective of the date of the acquisition, sale, or occurrence of the possibility to exercise the voting rights; or
- is notified of the latest changes in the company's registered capital.

In the event of a failure to comply with the above notification requirement, the SEC shall temporarily suspend the voting rights of the person in question. The relevant ruling shall remain in force until the relevant notification obligation has been fulfilled.

(xii) Dividends.

The general rule is that dividends are paid out of distributable profit. The payment of dividends is determined on the basis of a separate decision adopted at an ordinary meeting of the general assembly, by which the amount of the dividend and its payment deadline, which may not exceed a period of six months from the day of adopting the decision, shall be determined. It may be executed by payment of a monetary dividend or by payment of dividends in the form of a company's shares (only for joint-stock companies). In case of payment of dividend in company's shares, such payment must be authorized by shareholders whose class of shares is used for such payment. Further, under conditions stipulated by the Company Law (unless the relevant by-laws of the company in question provide otherwise), a company is allowed to pay a temporary/interim dividend at any time between the ordinary sessions of the general assembly (*privremena dividenda/ međudividenda*). These conditions are that: (i) business and financial reports prepared for this purpose clearly show that the company, in the period for which dividend is paid, has achieved a profit and the company's funds are sufficient for the payment of dividend; and (ii) the amount of the dividend is not above the profit achieved after the close of the previous business year for which the financial reports are prepared, increased by the amount of retained profit and the amount of reserves that can be used for this purpose, and decreased by the amount of determined losses and the amount to be placed in reserve in accordance with the law or the company's by-laws. Decision on payment of temporary/interim dividends may be reached by the general assembly of a company, or by the board of directors (in the case of the one-tier corporate governance structure) or by the supervisory board (in the case of a two-tier corporate governance structure) if stipulated by articles of association or a decision of the general assembly. If a temporary/interim dividend is paid on the basis of a decision of the board of directors or the supervisory board, it may be executed only as a monetary payment.

(xiii) Purchase of Own Shares.

Limited liability companies can acquire an own equity interest (*sopstveni udeo*) under certain mandatory conditions and on the basis of approval of the company's general assembly, provided that the company has more than one member and that by the acquisition of the ownership interest, the company will still have at least one other member after the acquisition of such ownership interest. Acquired own equity interest does not grant voting rights to a company, nor is it entitled to participate in the distribution of dividends. A company may distribute its own equity interest to company members in proportion to the share of their equity interests in the company's share capital, transfer its own equity interest to a company member or a third party against consideration (in which case each company member shall have a preemption right proportionate to the amount of his/her equity interest in the company).

A similar rule applies in the case of joint-stock companies. A number of conditions apply in the case of a company acquiring its own shares (e.g., the shares in question must be fully paid in, and, in the case of a public joint-stock company, if the total par value of shares (or their accounting value in case of non-par shares) thus acquired, including any own shares acquired earlier, does not exceed 10% of the company's share capital). However, in some exceptional cases, a prior general assembly approval may not be necessary for the acquisition of own shares (e.g., in the case of a public joint-stock company, if there is a need to prevent major and imminent damage to the company). In addition, acquiring of own shares by a joint-stock company in certain specific cases (e.g., as a result of the exercise of rights of dissenting shareholders or as a result of a court decision) does not fall under general limitations provided by the Company Law.

If own shares of a joint-stock company were acquired in a manner contrary to the applicable rules, a company would be obliged to dispose of them or annul them in the period of one year following the date of acquisition. However, even if a company acquired its own shares in accordance with the relevant rules, it may be obliged to dispose of/distribute them within certain deadlines depending on the purpose for which such acquisition took place. For example, in the case of a company's own shares that were acquired by such company for the purpose of their redistribution to the company's employees, such redistribution must be accomplished within one year of their acquisition by the company in question. Further, if the value of acquired own shares exceeds 10% of the company's share capital, a company would be obliged to dispose of such shares within three years of the date of acquisition so that the total value of own shares thus acquired does not exceed 10% of share capital.

In the event that a company fails to meet the relevant deadline, the company's board of directors or supervisory board (in the case of a two-tier corporate governance structure) is obliged to annul such shares immediately upon the expiration of the relevant deadline without a special decision and to decrease the company's registered basic capital accordingly.

(xiv) Piercing of the Corporate Veil.

The Company Law provides that a shareholder of a company which abuses the separate and independent legal and economic status of such a company becomes liable for the company's obligations. Circumstances which constitute the aforementioned abuse under the Company Law include, *inter alia*, the shareholder of the relevant company: (i) using the company to achieve a purpose which is prohibited; (ii) using or disposing of the company's assets as if they were the shareholder's own property; (iii) using the company or its assets in order to damage the company's creditors; and (iv) reducing the company's assets in order to obtain benefit for itself or for third parties, despite knowing (or being deemed to know) that the company would be unable to meet its obligations.

Where the corporate veil has been pierced in accordance with the above grounds, the company's creditors may file a claim against the shareholder in question to the competent court within six months of the date on which the creditor becomes aware of such abuse, but in any event not later than five years from the date of the alleged abuse taking place.

It should be noted that the case law in this area is relatively underdeveloped and it is not clear how difficult it may be to prove some of the above grounds and/or which other grounds may also be invoked as grounds to argue that a parent company/owner should be liable for the obligations of its subsidiary.

(xv) Insolvency.

As a general matter, under the Insolvency Act, which regulates and applies to insolvency proceedings for most of the company types (e.g., insolvency proceedings for banks and insurance companies are regulated pursuant to a different set of rules), an insolvency proceeding commences pursuant to a court's decision that is made on the basis of a proposal from the authorized parties (e.g., creditor, insolvency debtor), when at least one of the main reasons for insolvency is determined to be fulfilled in the course of the relevant court procedure.

The main grounds that trigger insolvency are a company's: (i) permanent inability to comply with its payment obligations (i.e., the company is unable to meet its pecuniary obligations within forty-five days of the day on which an obligation becomes due or completely suspends all payments for a continuous period of thirty days); (ii) threatened inability to comply with payment obligations (i.e., when a company makes probable that it will be unable to fulfil its pecuniary obligations when they become due); (iii) over-indebtedness (i.e., it exists if the company's assets are less than its obligations); and (iv) failure of a company to act in accordance with previously adopted reorganization plan (i.e., if a company does not act in accordance with the reorganization plan or act in a way which seriously jeopardizes execution of the reorganization plan) and if adoption of a reorganization plan was caused in a fraudulent or illegal manner. A presumption of permanent inability to comply with payment obligations arises if the proposal for the initiation of the insolvency proceeding has been made by a creditor who has previously failed to collect his/her/its receivables by any means of execution within the territory of Serbia. A creditor may initiate insolvency proceedings over its debtor for reasons stated under (i) and (iv) in this paragraph, while the debtor may initiate its own insolvency for all reasons stated in this paragraph.

If the insolvency proceeding is initiated, one of its main legal consequences is that representation and management competencies exercised by the insolvency debtor's general manager, other management/supervisory bodies, and/or proxies are transferred to the insolvency administrator appointed by the court, who starts to manage the day-to-day affairs of the insolvent company and the insolvency process itself. Similarly, the regular rights of the insolvency debtor's shareholders are also suspended. In addition, all collection procedures initiated against the insolvency debtor by its creditors, either judicial or extrajudicial, are suspended and could be continued only in accordance with rules on collection of receivables in the insolvency procedure. Such a rule applies regardless of the fact whether a receivable towards an insolvency debtor has been collateralized or not, but certain exceptions from it are possible. Namely, in case collateralized assets of an insolvency debtor have not been properly secured by an insolvency administrator, or if the value of collateralized assets is constantly decreasing and there is no possibility to prevent such decrease, or if collateralized assets are not of critical value for sale or reorganization of an insolvency debtor, the court may, upon a request of a secured creditor, allow enforcement and collection over such assets for a period of nine months. This period can be extended only once, for an additional period of three months and only if the creditor provides adequate evidence that enforcement or collection over such assets is underway.

In general, the insolvency proceeding leads to one of the following two outcomes: (i) the insolvent company is pronounced to be bankrupt and its assets are either sold separately or jointly (as the sale of entire business); or (ii) reorganization is approved for the insolvent company through which the company will continue to operate and repay the re-scheduled obligations (please note that the reorganization status may last up to five years, whereas individual obligations may be settled in a longer period). In the case of the first scenario, when the insolvent company's assets are being sold separately, the company will eventually be liquidated, and its shareholders may in theory receive some funds on account of their nominal stakes in the company. Such an outcome is rare in practice, as the relevant funds usually are not sufficient to provide compensation for all creditor classes in full.

In the event the insolvent company's assets will be sold together as a business, effectively, the entire company is sold to a buyer who becomes the new owner of the company. Such a company exits insolvency proceedings and may continue with its regular business activities, whereas creditors' claims are compensated from a bankruptcy estate in which the proceeds of the company's sale will be collected. In other words, the company and, indirectly, its new owner are insulated from the creditor claims that were made in the course of the insolvency process. This does not mean, however, that the company will be completely 'bullet-proof' against each and every potential claim that existed and/or was triggered prior to the insolvency process. Namely, some of these claims may be potentially brought against the company even after it exits insolvency, e.g., restitution claims on real estate owned by the bankruptcy debtor, raised in accordance with restitution regulations. Therefore, the prospective buyer of the company should consider the company's background and previous operations to assess the likelihood of any such claims being successfully entertained against the company.

As already noted above, insolvency proceedings may alternatively develop into a reorganization (i.e., novation of the debtor's obligations). Reorganization has to be based on a reorganization plan, which may be submitted prior to the opening of insolvency proceedings, as a so-called pre-packed reorganization plan, or after the opening of insolvency proceedings, as a regular reorganization plan. Regular reorganization plan may be proposed by the insolvency administrator, secured and unsecured creditors of the insolvency debtor, and shareholders holding at least 30% of the equity of the insolvency debtor, and there can be more than one proposal at a time. Pre-packed reorganization plan can be proposed only by the insolvency debtor, and there can be only one such proposal at the time. A variety of economic, financial and legal measures for the reorganization of the debtor company may be proposed, which, *inter alia*, include write-offs, transformation of debt into equity, granting grace period for debts, partial sale of property, taking new bank loans, etc. In order to be accepted, a proposed plan has to be adopted by the simple majority of the total amount of claims in each of the creditors' classes. If and when the adopted plan becomes final, it is treated as a multilateral contract between all creditors. A failure to act in accordance with the adopted plan is a reason for the initiation of a new insolvency procedure.

(xvi) Considerations Related to Liquidation of a Company.

The liquidation of a company is a proceeding envisaged under the Company Law for companies which have enough assets/funds to cover all their debts prior to their dissolution and is initiated by the general assembly of a company. If a company is in liquidation, a liquidation administrator may be appointed, and such person replaces the company's legal representatives. It is possible to appoint more than one liquidation administrator. In case a liquidation administrator is not appointed, all legal representatives of the company in question become liquidation administrators, and unless stipulated otherwise by a decision on liquidation, they jointly represent the company in liquidation. The liquidation manager is entitled, *inter alia*, to sell the company's property in order to cover the creditors' claims.

Some of the main consequences of the initiation of a liquidation proceeding are that dividends are not paid to the shareholders and the remaining assets of the company are not distributed to the shareholders until claims of all creditors are paid in full. However, if from the initial liquidation balance sheet, it is determined that the company's assets are not sufficient to cover claims of all of the company's creditors, the liquidation administrator is obliged, within a certain mandatory timeframe, to submit to the court a proposal for the commencement of insolvency proceedings. In such a case, the liquidation administrator is not entitled to cover the claims of the company's creditors.

(xvii) Choice of Law.

The freedom to choose governing law, jurisdiction and arbitration (both international and domestic) is generally recognized and enforceable under Serbian law. There are, of course, certain exceptions such as in matters involving real property or in the context of family affairs. Also, in certain cases, it is not quite clear whether foreign law, courts and/or arbitration may agree to govern and adjudicate disputes arising from a contractual relationship or a part thereof, which is a source of considerable legal uncertainty.

A large number of foreign laws governed contracts have been concluded in Serbia, especially since the commencement of transition approximately twenty years ago. Also, even when they are being governed by Serbian law, many contracts in the M&A area are being concluded pursuant to international and, especially, Anglo-Saxon precedents. Potentially, a number of provisions in such contracts (irrespective of whether the contractual choice of law is Serbian or foreign) may be problematic from the point of view of mandatory norms of Serbian law. However, to the best of our knowledge, the court practice around such issues is undeveloped and thus it is very difficult to anticipate the outcome of any such proceeding.

In the event that a contractual relationship is governed by a foreign law and such choice of law is not contrary to the applicable Serbian rules, Serbian courts are supposed to determine and apply foreign law as a matter of course (i.e., ex officio). In this context, Serbian courts may ask the Serbian Ministry of Justice to obtain texts of foreign laws or applicable court practices in the event such documents are not available to the domestic courts (which is likely to be the case in this context). As a general matter, it is fair to say that Serbian courts are not experienced in applying foreign laws and thus it would be prudent that foreign law clauses are accompanied by the choice of an appropriate foreign judicial or arbitral forum to the extent this is not contrary to the mandatory norms of the Serbian law.

2.7 Specific Rules on Public Takeovers

2.7.1 Takeover Law: Applicability

[92] Public takeovers (mandatory and voluntary takeovers) are regulated by the Takeover Law. The Takeover Law applies to takeovers of joint-stock companies with their seat in Serbia. The Takeover Law further stipulates that a joint-stock company may be considered a target company for the purpose of takeover only if at least one of the following two conditions is met:

(1) its shares are traded on a regulated market (which is currently only the Stock Exchange)/MTP in Serbia; and/or
(2) it has more than one hundred shareholders on every last day of the month over three consecutive months and has total capital in the amount of at least EUR3 m.

[93] In other words, the Takeover Law will apply to takeovers of non-public joint-stock companies that are not listed or whose shares are not otherwise traded in an organized market in Serbia if the above criteria regarding the number of shareholders and minimum capital are fulfilled.

2.7.2 General Takeover Principles

[94] The Takeover Law stipulates the following six general principles that must be complied with in the course of each takeover:

(i) all of the target company's shareholders have an equal position in the takeover process;
(ii) when a person acquires control in a company, other shareholders in such company must be protected so that they can sell their shares to the bidder under the same conditions;
(iii) the target company's shareholders must be fully, accurately, and in a timely fashion informed regarding the takeover bid in order to have sufficient time to correctly evaluate the bid, determine their interests, and decide to accept or reject the takeover bid;
(iv) during the takeover process, the target company's management is obliged to act in the best interests of the target company's shareholders;
(v) the bidder and the target company are obliged to carry out the takeover process within the shortest possible period of time so that the target company is not hindered in its business operations for a longer period than necessary; and
(vi) the bidder and other persons participating in the takeover process must not create by their activities any market distortions which would result in an artificial increase or decrease in the price of the target company's shares.

[95] Also, the Takeover Law contains a number of exceptions to the requirement to launch a takeover bid. Some of these exceptions include situations in which the takeover bid would be unwarranted because the acquisition of shares was a consequence of another legal process, such as inheritance, changes to the company's legal form, a merger or bankruptcy, or situations in which the Serbian state (or its agencies) is selling shares it holds in banks, insurance companies and other commercial entities.

2.7.3 Mandatory Takeover Bid

[96] In Serbia, the concept of mandatory (i.e., where a shareholder has passed certain thresholds of share ownership and must make a bid for the rest of the company's shares) and voluntary takeover bids are recognized.

[97] The general rule is that a takeover bid must be launched by a person who has acquired, directly or indirectly, solely or by acting in concert, shares that, together with the shares that the person has already acquired, exceed the threshold of 25% of the target company's voting shares (the so-called control threshold).

[98] After the initial acquisition of 25% of shares and launching of takeover bid, the same acquirer is obliged to make a new takeover bid only after it acquires at least an additional 10% of the total issued voting shares of the target or when, irrespective of the number of additionally acquired shares, further acquisition of shares results in the acquirer holding more than 75% of the total issued voting shares of the target. However, there is no obligation for the acquirer to launch a mandatory takeover bid in case of further acquisition of shares of the target company after it acquires, based on a takeover bid, at least 75% of the voting shares.

2.7.4 Voluntary Takeover Bid

[99] A party can launch a voluntary takeover bid even if it is not obliged to launch a mandatory takeover bid under conditions and in a manner prescribed by the Takeover Law. In such a case, the prospective buyer has to first publish a so-called notification of takeover intent containing the same information as is required for the takeover bid itself. The publication of the notification creates an obligation for the bidder to publish the relevant takeover bid. The Takeover Law stipulates that only a voluntary takeover bid may be conditional (i.e., that a bidder states in a takeover bid that it seeks to acquire a certain minimum number or percentage of the target company's voting shares as the condition for the takeover bid to oblige it).

2.7.5 Takeover Bid Procedure

[100]

(i) Notification Requirements.
After acquiring the relevant number of voting shares that triggers an obligation to launch the takeover bid process, the acquirer must, without delay but not later than two business days following the day on which the obligation to launch a takeover bid arose, publish a notification of the takeover intent and submit such notification simultaneously to the relevant regulated market/MTP where the shares of the target company are traded, the Central Register, the SEC and the target company.
The acquirer must publish the notification of takeover intent in the same manner in which it will subsequently publish the actual takeover bid. Such notification must contain the same information as that which is to be included in the actual takeover bid (e.g., the price that the bidder shall pay per share, the term and manner of payment for the shares, and the validity period of the takeover bid).

(ii) Request for Approval of Publication of the Takeover Bid.
The SEC is in charge of overseeing the takeover process and is the main regulatory body in this area. According to the Takeover Law, the SEC is, *inter alia*, in charge of issuing the approval of the publication of the takeover bid after the relevant documents are filed by the bidder.
Within fifteen business days of the day on which the obligation to launch the takeover bid has arisen, the bidder must file with the SEC the following main documents:

- request for approval to publish the takeover bid;
- takeover bid;
- short-form takeover bid; and
- text of the (previously published) notification of the takeover intent.

(iii) SEC's Decision-Making Process.

The general deadline for the SEC to issue its approval of the application to publish the takeover bid is ten business days. However, this period can be extended up to ten business days in the event that the SEC needs to cooperate with the relevant anti-monopoly, anti-money laundering (AML), or other bodies with a view to 'preventing disturbances on the capital market in Serbia'.

The SEC shall issue the approval after it establishes:

- that the information contained in the takeover bid and the documents appended to the application for approval of the bid are complete and true;
- that the price in the takeover bid has been determined in accordance with applicable rules; and
- that if the bid is modified to increase the price, the bidder has secured the settlement funds.

When deciding on whether it will approve or reject the takeover bid or its amendment, the SEC shall not assess the justifiability and reasonableness of the elements of the takeover bid but merely the formal compliance with the applicable rules.

(iv) Bid Publication and Submission.

The bidder must publish the short-form takeover bid immediately after receiving the SEC's approval of the request to publish the takeover bid. The publication must be made in one daily newspaper that covers the whole territory of Serbia. The bidder must immediately submit to the SEC a copy of the published short-form takeover bid.

The bidder must also submit, no later than the day on which it orders the publication of the short-form takeover bid in the newspaper, a copy of the approved takeover bid to:

- the target company;
- the relevant regulated market/MTP where the shares of the target company are traded; and
- the Central Register.

Furthermore, the bidder is obliged to submit a copy of the approved takeover bid to all shareholders of the target company within three days of the day on which it orders the publication of the short-form takeover bid in the newspaper. Once it receives the SEC's decision on the approval of the bidder's application to publish the takeover bid, the Central Register is obliged to allow the bidder to access data concerning the target company's shareholders, as well as to publish the takeover bid on its Internet page.

(v) Bid Duration.

The bid duration period is calculated from the day on which the short-form takeover bid is published in the relevant newspaper. The minimum takeover bid duration is twenty-one days, while the maximum is set at forty-five days.

However, the latter period can be extended due to changes in the takeover bid or as a result of a counter-takeover bid. In the case of changes to the takeover bid (which are allowed only if they improve the initial takeover bid, that is, if the price in the takeover bid is raised and/or a condition in the conditional takeover bid is removed), the takeover bid's duration is extended by seven days, but the absolute bid duration period may not be longer than sixty days. In the case of counter-takeover bid(s), the total period for both the original and the subsequent counter-takeover bid(s) cannot exceed seventy days from the day on which the short-form takeover bid of the initial bidder is published.

2.7.6 Takeover Bid Price

[101] The Takeover Law stipulates two main rules for the calculation of the minimum takeover price (depending on the 'liquidity' of the target company's shares). In addition to these, the Takeover Law stipulates certain additional rules for the calculation of the share price that will apply instead of the previous two, irrespective of whether the shares in question are deemed to be liquid or not:

(i) The Formula for Liquid Shares.
Shares in the target company are considered to be liquid when their trading volume within the period of six months preceding the acquisition of the controlling threshold was equal to at least 0.5% of all issued voting shares of the company, provided that in the course of the total of at least three calendar months within such six-month period at least 0.05% of all issued voting shares of the company in question were traded in the course of more than one-third of all trading days each month.
If shares in a target company are considered to be liquid according to the criteria explained above, the bidder is obliged to offer, at the minimum, the highest of the following prices:
- the weighted average price of voting shares in the period of six months preceding the date when the mandatory takeover bid obligation is triggered; such price is to be determined on the basis of the trading reports on the regulated market/MTP; and
- the highest price at which the bidder or the persons acting in concert with the bidder acquired shares in the period of twelve months preceding the date when the obligation to launch the bid was triggered, including the price paid for the acquisition of the shares which triggered the obligation to launch the takeover bid.

(ii) The Formula for Non-Liquid Shares.
If the target company's shares do not fulfil the criteria for the purpose of being qualified as liquid shares or are not traded on the relevant regulated market/MTP, the bidder is obliged to offer to the target company's shareholders at least the highest of the following values:
- the highest of the prices for the shares of the target company for which the bidder or person acting in concert with the bidder acquired shares in

the period of twelve months preceding the day on which the launching of the mandatory bid is triggered;
  - the book value of the target company's voting shares according to the last annual financial statements of the target; or
  - the fair value of the target company's voting shares, calculated on the day on which the launching of a mandatory takeover bid is triggered.

(iii) Additional Rules Relating to Minimum Share Price.
If the bidder, or persons acting in concert with the bidder, who previously acquired at least 25% shares in the target company in the process of privatization or in other specific cases that are exempt from the obligation to launch a takeover bid, further acquire shares of the target company within two years following the initial acquisition of voting shares of the target company, it is obliged to launch a mandatory takeover bid process and to offer the price that is not lower than the price it had paid for the initially acquired shares.

If the bidder, or the persons acting in concert with the bidder, acquire or dispose of the target company's voting shares during the takeover process (i.e., from the moment at which the controlling threshold is reached) outside of such takeover process for a price higher than the price described in preceding sections, the bidder is obliged to offer such higher price in the takeover bid.

(iv) The Form in Which the Price for Shares Is Paid.
The consideration for the target company's shares may be offered in cash, or in the form of securities regulated by the Capital Markets Law or debt securities issued by the Serbian state and NBS.

Shares have to fulfil certain conditions in order to be offered as consideration. Namely, they must:
  - be of the same type and class as the shares subject to the takeover bid;
  - be admitted to the relevant securities market, which is of at least the same level of transparency as the market on which the shares subject to the bid are admitted; and
  - not be encumbered.

Where both the cash and shares are offered as consideration, the bidder shall be free to determine the ratio between the cash and shares.

2.7.7 Passing Control to the Buyer

[102] A shareholder of a target company shall accept the bid by depositing with the Central Register the shares which are the subject of the takeover bid prior to the expiry of the validity period of the bid. If a shareholder has deposited shares in accordance with the requirements provided in the takeover bid, the acceptance of the takeover bid and the payment obligation shall become effective upon expiry of the validity period of the takeover bid.

[103] The bidder may not take over the deposited shares, and/or the deposited shares may not be transferred to the bidder prior to the expiry of the validity period of the bid and before the shares are paid, which shall be determined by the Central Register.

2.7.8 Takeover Bid Consequences

[104]

(i) Voting Rights.
From the day on which the notification of takeover intent is published until the day of the publication of the takeover report (which the bidder is obliged to publish within one business day following the expiration of the bid period and the expiration of the deadline for the payment of tendered shares) the shares owned by the bidder, as well as persons acting in concert with the bidder, do not carry any voting rights.

(ii) Prohibition on Advertising and Influence on Shareholders.
Following the bid's publication, there is a strict prohibition against the exercising, either directly or through advertising, of any influence on the target company's shareholders by offering or promising gifts, services, or other benefits. The prohibition extends to the bidder, the target company, and the boards of directors and shareholders of both the target company and the bidder, as well as to third parties.

(iii) Prohibition on Publication of a New Notification of Takeover Intent.
Following the bid's publication, no third party can publish a notification of takeover intent regarding the same target company. Such a third party is only permitted to potentially publish a counter-takeover bid.

(iv) Limited Reasons for the Bid's Withdrawal.
The bidder may withdraw the bid only due to the following limited reasons:
- publication of a counter-takeover bid with a higher share price; or
- the target company's bankruptcy.

The bidder is obliged to immediately notify the SEC, the target company, and the Central Register regarding its withdrawal of the takeover bid.

(v) Prohibition on Trading in Shares.
Until the expiry of the bid's period, the bidder, as well as persons acting in concert with the bidder, are prohibited from purchasing or agreeing to purchase the target company's shares in any manner other than through the takeover bid. Similarly, the bidder must not sell or agree to sell shares of the target company. Exceptionally, the bidder, as well as persons acting in concert with the bidder, may sell shares in specific cases where the bidder or persons acting in concert with the bidder acquired the shares of the target company without launching the mandatory takeover bid.

2.7.9 Consequences of Takeover Rules' Breaches

[105] If a person under a duty to announce an offer fails to announce the offer within the imposed time period, the SEC will either order that person to announce the offer or (if a person has no funds to finance the offer) order the sale of an appropriate number of shares within three months. The SEC will inform the Central Register that such shares carry no voting rights (until they are sold).

2.7.10 Target Company's Obligations

[106] From the moment of the publication of the notification of the takeover intent until the completion of the takeover bid process, the target company's board of directors may not:

- increase the target company's share capital;
- cause the target company to undertake extraordinary actions or enter into an agreement that would significantly alter the status of the target company's property or liabilities;
- cause the target company to buy or sell treasury shares; and/or
- publish a takeover bid for another company.

without the prior consent of the target company's general assembly, which may decide on such issues with a simple majority of votes.

[107] Within the same period of time, the target company must not amend its articles of association so as to limit the number of votes carried by its voting shares. However, in the event that such limitations already exist in this document, the target company's general assembly can abolish such provisions with a simple majority of votes.

[108] Not later than ten days following the bid's publication, the relevant corporate body of the target company is required to publish its opinion with respect to the takeover bid and state the facts that support such opinion in the same manner as that in which the takeover bid was published. Simultaneously with the aforementioned opinion, the opinion of a representative of the target company's employees should also be published if such opinion was provided in the course of a special procedure prescribed by the Takeover Law.

[109] In addition, within the takeover bid period, the target company's board of directors is authorized to call for a counter-takeover bid.

2.7.11 Squeeze-Outs and Mandatory Buy-Outs

[110] The process of squeeze-outs and mandatory buy-outs is regulated by the Company Law. The relevant squeeze-out threshold is 90% of shares (representing 90% of the company's basic capital and granting at least 90% of votes of all voting shares). In addition to this, the squeeze-out needs to be formally approved by the general assembly of the relevant company whose minority shareholders are being squeezed out.

[111] The company is obliged to determine the share price in the decision on squeeze-out in accordance with the detailed rules prescribed by the Company Law and to file such decision with the SBRA for registration within three days. Following registration of the decision on squeeze-out, the company is obliged to deliver such decision to the Central Register within three days, or the decision in question will cease to be valid. Within a further period of three days, the majority shareholder has an obligation to deposit the funds necessary for the payment of the relevant share price into a special account opened with the Central Register. Following the expiration of the previous deadline, the Central Register should finalize the squeeze-out procedure (i.e., settlement).

[112] In the case of mandatory buy-outs, the majority shareholder who holds shares that represent at least 90% of that company's basic capital is obliged to purchase the shares of any minority shareholder upon the written request of such shareholder, which must be addressed to the company in which the relevant shares are held (but it should be considered that the request is also addressed to the majority shareholder by virtue of law). Within a period of sixty days of the day of the receipt of such request, the company in question is obliged to determine the share price in accordance with the same rules that apply to the determination of the squeeze-out price and to inform the majority and selling shareholders of such share price. The latter is further obliged to pay the relevant price within thirty days of the receipt of the aforementioned information about the purchase price.

2.7.12 Stake-Building

[113] In general, the key shareholding thresholds that a bidder will have in mind when considering stake-building are 10% (which is sufficient to block another bidder from using the statutory compulsory squeeze-out procedure in relation to shareholders who have not accepted a takeover offer) and 25% as the latter would trigger a mandatory bid under the Takeover Law.

[114] With respect to disclosure obligations and reporting duties related to the acquisition of a stake which is not subject to the mandatory bid, the Capital Markets Law stipulates that a person who/that directly or indirectly reaches, exceeds or falls under 5%, 10%, 15%, 20%, 25%, 30%, 50% and 75% of the voting rights in a joint-stock company whose shares are traded on a regulated market/MTP, is obliged to notify the company in question of such fact and also the SEC and the regulated market/MTP on which the shares of such company are traded (for further information on general reporting duties, *see* paragraph **[40]**).

2.7.13 Takeover Timetable

[115] The takeover process itself lasts approximately between two and three months, including possible extensions of the offer period. The relevant timing will depend on whether a competing takeover offer will be launched. However, in practice, in Serbia, thus far, this has been a relatively rare occurrence. Also, the timing depends on the time needed by the Competition Authority to review and approve the relevant merger filing that needs to be submitted to this body in relation to each takeover offer.

2.7.14 Deal Protection

[116] The applicable rules in Serbia do not regulate the issue of so-called break fees. Thus, it is unclear if such fees could be offered and paid in practice.

2.8 Other Relevant Laws and Due Diligence Issues

2.8.1 Anti-bribery and Anti-corruption

[117] Corruption remains one of the most serious problems of Serbian society. There seems to be an increased readiness within the Serbian Government to tackle this issue in a more radical manner and the fight against corruption is almost at the top of its publicly stated priorities. In 2018, Serbia started to implement new regulations on competencies and authorities of state bodies in combating corruption, introducing four special prosecutors and four special divisions of high courts, which are exclusively competent to process, *inter alia,* all criminal offences with corruptive elements in the territory of Serbia. In addition, a number of new methods for combating corruption were introduced, such as establishing specialized task forces and financial forensic departments with competent bodies. Also, as of 1 September 2020, the new Law on Preventing Corruption applies, introducing a new set of obligations for public officials and state bodies, such as prohibition for public officials to use information not previously disclosed to the general public or additional reporting obligations to the Anti-Corruption Agency.

[118] However, discovering and punishing previous misdeeds is just one part of this battle and the Serbian Government has yet to seriously commence actions to prevent and fight against new corruption.

[119] From the M&A perspective, it is important to note that under the Law on the Liability of Legal Entities for Criminal Offences, any legal entity (with the exception of the state and its administrative subdivisions) can be held liable for criminal offences. This law applies to all crimes that are prescribed under the Criminal Code and under other laws if the conditions governing liability of legal entities for criminal offences stipulated by this law are satisfied. The liability of legal entities for criminal offences is based upon the culpability of the responsible person within the company. The responsible person is defined as a natural person who is legally or de facto entrusted with certain duties within a legal entity, as well as a person authorized or who may be considered to have been authorized to act on behalf of the legal entity. A legal entity can be criminally liable for acts committed by a responsible person within such person's power or authorization to the benefit of the legal entity in question.

[120] Liability of legal entities for criminal offences also exists where a lack of supervision or control on the part of the responsible person allowed the execution of the criminal offence to the benefit of that legal entity by a natural person operating under the supervision and control of the responsible person. In addition, a

legal entity may be criminally liable for criminal offences committed by the responsible person even if criminal proceedings against such person have been suspended or charges have been dismissed.

[121] The following are the penalties and protective measures that can be imposed against companies in the above context:

- dissolution of a legal entity;
- monetary fine;
- suspended sentence;
- suspended sentence (during the term of which the company in question is placed under 'protective supervision');
- seizure of objects (objects used or intended to be used for committing a criminal offence or obtained as a result of a criminal offence);
- prohibition of certain activities; and/or
- publication of the relevant judgment.

[122] The 'long reach' of the United States (US) Foreign Corrupt Practices Act (FCPA) and the United Kingdom (UK) Bribery Act has had an increased impact on M&A transactions in Serbia. This in particular relates to companies that are subject to the FCPA and the UK Bribery Act due to their seat or otherwise. Namely, such companies (including their domestic subsidiaries) have become increasingly concerned and seek to identify in respect of their partners/targets any circumstances, which could subsequently trigger their liability under the aforementioned laws.

2.8.2 Money Laundering Regulations

[123] The main source of the specialized rules against money laundering in Serbia is the Law on the Prevention of Money Laundering and Financing of Terrorism. Also, in 2015, the Serbian Government adopted a national AML and counter-terrorism financing (AML/CFT) strategy containing recommendations for the enhancement of the existing AML and AML/CFT system by identifying and analyzing the legislative, institutional and operational AML/CFT framework. A number of institutions take part in AML/CFT activities in Serbia and are classified into three groups:

(i) *obliged entities* – all those entities that are required to apply legislation governing the prevention of money laundering (banks, insurance companies, auditors, etc.). Such entities should apply actions and measures set out in the Law on the Prevention of Money Laundering and Financing of Terrorism. Please note that lawyers are also required to apply the actions and measures set forth in the aforementioned law, which is a source of some uncertainties as to the scope of application of legal privilege that should otherwise apply fairly broadly to the client-attorney communications;

(ii) *competent supervisors* – authorities such as the Administration for the Prevention of Money Laundering (APML), NBS, SEC and Tax Administration. Their role is to control and ensure the proper application of the AML/CFT legislation; and

(iii) *police, prosecutor's office and courts* – who are responsible for the enforcement and sanctioning of the breaches of the AML/CFT framework.

[124] The central AML/CFT body in the system is the APML, which is responsible for the implementation of the Law on the Prevention of Money Laundering and Terrorism Financing. The Administration collects, analyses, and stores data and information obtained from the so-called obliged entities mentioned above. When it suspects that money laundering has occurred in a transaction or in relation to an individual or entity, the Administration notifies the competent state authorities (police, etc.) so that they can undertake actions and measures within their competence.

2.8.3 Environmental Laws and Regulations

[125] The environmental legal framework in Serbia comprises over 100 laws and regulations. Many of these laws and regulations have already been harmonized with the relevant EU rules. However, a number of rules are yet to be brought in line with the EU framework. What is even more important is that the underlying practice is lagging behind even the relevant domestic standards. Namely, according to the initial assessments of the level of Serbia's compliance with the applicable EU standards that are conducted as a part of Serbia's ongoing accession process, the environment is one of the areas in which Serbia has the lowest level of compliance with EU standards and practice.

[126] The umbrella law in the field of environmental safety is the Law on Environmental Protection. This law regulates the integral system of environmental protection in the country, which aims to realize the human right to live and develop in a healthy environment and to find a balance between economic development and environmental protection. In addition, there are a number of laws/regulations which regulate environmental protection in fields such as the assessment of the impact of plans, programmes and projects on the environment; the integrated prevention and control of pollution; the protection of nature; the protection of air, water, soil, forests and geological resources; the management of chemicals, ionizing and non-ionizing radiation; waste management; and the prevention of noise and vibration.

[127] In light of the above, depending on the type of activities/business of the potential acquisition target, it should be carefully ascertained which environmental laws might apply and which relevant issues could arise under such laws that should subsequently be assessed through a due diligence process. In addition to the relevant regulatory analyses that are conducted by legal advisors, investors should also engage specialized technical advisors, especially in case the target operates in an industry that has a considerable environmental impact.

2.8.4 Registration, Enforcement and Protection of IP Rights

[128] Serbian Intellectual Property (IP) rights' framework is largely in line with applicable international/EU rules in this field. The Intellectual Property Office

(IPO) is the main institution responsible for tasks related to IP rights (patents, trademarks, industrial designs, indications of geographical origin and topographies of integrated circuits). The IPO is responsible for the conduct of administrative procedures for the granting of patents, trademarks, industrial designs, indications of geographical origin and topographies of integrated circuits. As regards copyright and related rights, the IPO is in charge of monitoring the developments in this field and preparing draft regulations, as well as in charge of the administrative supervision of the work of organizations for the collective management of copyright and related rights.

[129] Transfers of industrial property rights generally require registration in the relevant public register held within the IPO. A transfer is undertaken on the basis of a written agreement on transfer, which should have certain mandatory elements. However, in order for such transfer to take effect, registration at the relevant IPO register is required.

[130] Note that all public registries of industrial property rights are held by the IPO, which is, as already noted above, also in charge of conducting the administrative procedure under which relevant industrial property rights are granted. After an entry in the relevant registry has been made, the IPO issues a certificate to the owner of the relevant industrial property right. Please note that the IPO publishes an official gazette, which is issued bimonthly and contains information on applications for patents, inventions and granted industrial property rights.

[131] The registries of industrial property rights held by the IPO are available to the general public and each person can review information kept there. Furthermore, information from these registries is accessible via the IPO's website.

[132] Enforcement of IP rights is done through administrative and judicial authorities. The main administrative authorities in charge of enforcement are the customs and market inspectorate and inspections. In addition, the Ministry of the Interior has a special department devoted to fighting crimes against IP rights.

[133] Furthermore, the Law on Special Powers for the Efficient Protection of IP Rights sets out special powers of the competent authorities with the objective of securing efficient protection of IP rights. The competent authorities may, on their own initiative or upon the request of the holder of IP rights, temporarily confiscate goods or prohibit the performance of certain activities. However, goods may be permanently confiscated and destroyed only on the basis of a court decision or on the basis of a decision taken by the competent authority in cases envisaged by this law.

[134] Based on available practice, it appears that the relevant police department is quite agile in protecting various IP rights, especially when duly informed about the alleged infringement. However, the Serbian judiciary does not appear to hold the necessary experience and knowledge to deal with these types of legal issues which may create uncertainties and suboptimal results at this stage of protection of IP rights.

2.8.5 Mandatory Compensations/Indemnities for Agents and Other Distributors

[135] Serbia does not have a legal framework that focuses exclusively on distribution agreements. Also, the general rules currently in force do not provide for any mandatory compensation or other indemnity for agents/distributors arising from termination.

2.8.6 Valuation of Intangible Assets

[136] The valuation of intangible assets is undertaken by court-appointed experts. A number of issues may arise in the context of such valuations. For example, it is often difficult to attach a concrete value to ownership interests that are held in Serbian limited liability companies as such stakes are not publicly traded and thus do not have a market value. In particular, difficulties arise when the process is somewhat adversarial (e.g., pledge enforcement) and the company in question does not want to provide relevant business, financial, accounting, tax and other information that is needed to complete such valuation. This may give rise to a need to request the requisite level of cooperation from courts, which would likely result in further prolongation of the process.

2.8.7 'Change of Control' Clauses

[137] Change of control clauses are relatively common in the context of loan agreements that are concluded in Serbia. They can cover direct or indirect change of control, as well as require prior approval or merely notification following the relevant change. It is common for pre-acquisition due diligence analysis to pay substantial attention to determining the existence of such clauses in relevant target contracts. In addition to loan arrangements, such clauses can be found in a number of other contract types (e.g., business cooperation agreements).

2.9 The Due Diligence Process

[138] The due diligence process is nowadays a common pre-acquisition stage in Serbia. Purchasers normally carry out an investigation of the legal, financial, technological and environmental position of a target, as well as all relevant and related circumstances, and the majority of sellers understand the need to complete such analysis.

[139] A legal due diligence is generally conducted once the seller has committed to selling the target and the purchaser has expressed a strong interest in acquiring the target, often by signing either a 'letter of intent' or a 'memorandum of understanding' or has submitted a preliminary non-binding offer based on initial information provided by the seller and has, on the basis of such offer, been granted exclusivity for negotiations with the seller for a certain period of time. At this stage, all relevant legal relationships, the validity of existing agreements, and other legal matters must be clarified so that a final decision in respect of the acquisition may be taken.

[140] Historically, the due diligence process was conducted in the form of physical data rooms. However, for some time already, it has been the market standard that virtual data rooms are organized for the purpose of a due diligence process even if prospective targets are relatively small. Some exceptions occur in relation to extremely sensitive documents which are in certain cases offered for review in the form of the so-called physical 'red' data rooms.

2.9.1 Issues to Be Addressed in a Due Diligence Process

[141]

(i) General Remarks.
As already mentioned above, during the due diligence process, certain documents and information are disclosed to the prospective purchaser and/or its professional advisors. In doing so, various legal restrictions must be observed. Thus, an investor will typically gain access to certain information only after it has committed itself to comply with confidentiality obligations undertaken by the target company in order to avoid the abuse or disclosure of such information by the prospective purchaser or its professional advisors and to limit any damage that could be caused by such breach. These measures are commonly set out in the form of a confidentiality agreement concluded between the target company and the purchaser/its professional advisors and in the form of binding data room rules. Such agreements are market standard in Serbia.

(ii) Business Secrets.
Business secrets generally comprise information which is not commonly available or easily accessible in business circles, which derives commercial value from their secrecy and whose holder has undertaken reasonable measures so that they are kept confidential. In the course of due diligence, a reviewer will usually encounter business secrets of the target company, as well as business secrets pertaining to entities in contractual (or other) relationships with the target company.

It is within the sole discretion of the target company whether its business secrets will be disclosed to the prospective purchaser; in such case, the target company will determine the terms and conditions governing such disclosure.

In relation to information classified as a business secret by third parties, unless the latter consent to data disclosure, the target company should ensure a level of protection corresponding to the scope of protection it owes to the respective third party.

(iii) Personal Data Protection.
The term 'personal data' refers to any information relating to an individual, regardless of: (i) the form in which it is expressed or the medium which

carries it; (ii) on whose order, on whose behalf, or in whose interest that data is stored; (iii) the date of the data's creation; (iv) the place where the data is stored; (v) the method of obtaining data; or (vi) other characteristics of such data. A target company is entitled to disclose personal data based on the consent of the relevant individual or in cases where an exemption is stipulated by the applicable legislation (e.g., in the event of a court order). Since the relevant rules provide for no exceptions from the personal data protection obligations in the case of a due diligence process, such protection must be ensured by the target company and potentially other relevant parties.

(iv) Banking Secrets.
Under the Banking Law, all information related to a person, information on banking transactions and financial services of banks (including account balances and deposits), as well as ownership rights and business ties of its customers, shall be handled as banking secrets. This applies to information concerning both natural and legal persons.

Generally, a bank is prohibited from providing information considered to constitute a banking secret without its customer's consent unless a specific exemption stipulated by the Banking Law applies (e.g., a request made by the competent state authorities). As there is neither a special regulation nor a specific exemption in respect of the disclosure of banking secrets within the scope of the due diligence process, measures must be adopted to ensure an adequate level of protection for any disclosed information.

(v) Other Restrictions.
The applicable legal framework in Serbia protects a number of other categories of information. For example, in the context of capital markets regulations, privileged information is placed under a special regime aimed at preventing insider trading. Also, rules pertaining to investment funds prohibit the disclosure of data concerning an investment fund, its prospective activities and business plans, or any other information of relevance to the activities of such investment fund.

2.9.2 Relationship Between the Formal Due Diligence Process and the Imposition of Contractual Representations, Warranties and Indemnities

[142] Typically, one of the major deficiencies of any due diligence process is that the material disclosure will often be limited, especially at the initial stages of the due diligence process. This is the practice that is pursued not only by purely domestic companies but also by experienced Western advisors and is aimed at forcing the seller to make an investment decision based on limited facts.

[143] The concept of representations and warranties, as applied under English law, is not fully recognized under Serbian law, but they are used in share purchase agreements (SPAs) governed by Serbian or foreign law for a similar purpose. The purpose of representations is to provide the party in whose favour the representations are made with reasonable assurance that it may rely on certain facts when considering its intention to enter into an agreement and that if any such fact turns out to be incorrect, it will be compensated for the loss it has suffered due to its reliance upon it. The intended effect can be achieved by: (i) an express statement in the SPA that the party making such representations acknowledges and accepts the other party's reliance on such representations when signing the agreement; and (ii) an express obligation to put the recipient of the representation in the same position as it would have been in if the representation had been true, accurate and not misleading.

[144] A common law warranty is a term of the contract, and its breach constitutes a breach of the contract. However, Serbian law does not employ the terms 'terms of contract' or 'breach of contract'. Instead, it refers to the obligations of the parties under a contract and the breach of an obligation by a party. A pure statement of fact cannot, under Serbian law, be considered to constitute a contractual obligation. Therefore, to achieve the desired effect, that is, that a breach of warranties leads to a claim for damages or to a price reduction, an express obligation needs to be stipulated in the agreement that will oblige one party to put the recipient of the warranties in the same position as the recipient of the warranties would have been if the warranty was true, accurate and not misleading. Additionally, the Law on Contracts and Torts provides for the *ex lege* liability of the seller in case of certain physical and/or deficiencies in title.

2.10 Role of the Courts

2.10.1 Court Resolution of Disputes or Arbitration

[145] Subject to certain mandatory rules and exceptions, the parties to a commercial agreement may generally agree to refer their disputes to general courts or to arbitral tribunals (domestic or foreign). However, since difficulty in obtaining effective and timely legal protection from the Serbian courts is one of the well-recognized problems of the Serbian judicial system, parties to a dispute frequently appoint a local or foreign arbitral tribunal as the choice of forum.

2.10.2 Court Dispute Resolution

[146] As already mentioned, the duration of court proceedings is one of the weaknesses of the Serbian judicial system. In accordance with the data provided in the Annual Report on the Work of the Courts in the Republic of Serbia for 2020 of the Supreme Court of Cassation, it appears that the time needed for disposition of the cases, in general, is slowly but gradually improving. For example, in 2012, the average time needed for disposition of a case in Serbian courts was 534 days and 3 158 400 cases were pending before Serbian courts; in 2018, the required time was 270 days and 1 701 580 cases were pending; and in 2020, the required time was only 274 days, but only 1 510 472 cases were pending. However, it does not appear that all parts of the Serbian judicial system are improving at the same rate or at all. For example, the average disposition time of the Supreme Court of Cassation increased from 98 days in 2012 to 181 days in 2018 and 282 days in 2020, whereas the average disposition time of the Commercial Appellate Court decreased from 190 days in 2012 to 159 days in 2018 but again increased in 2020 to 185 days. On the other side, first instance commercial courts are continuously decreasing the average disposition time for first instance commercial cases, from 207 days in 2012 to 160 days in 2018 and 107 days in 2020.[2]

[147] However, it seems that there has been an increased political will to improve the Serbian judicial system in recent years. This was especially demonstrated by the adoption of the Law on Protection of Right to a Trial within a Reasonable Time, which provisions grant a right to trial within a reasonable time to every party in court proceedings, including enforcement proceedings, to every party in non-litigious proceedings and to the injured party in criminal proceedings. Remedies that parties may exercise in order to achieve their right to trial in a reasonable time-frame are a request to accelerate the process, which is submitted to the court in charge of the case, and a request for an equitable remuneration, which may be submitted to the State Attorney's Office and by which a monetary compensation and right to publication of a breach of the right in the press may be required. In addition to this, the Law on Enforcement and Security seeks to achieve a balance between the speed and effectiveness of enforcement proceedings while removing uncertainties that have emerged in practice. One of the methods by which it tries to achieve such goals is delegation of almost all types of enforcement procedures into the competence of private bailiffs.

[148] The aforementioned measures produced some tangible results since extensive court practice in relation to protecting rights to trial within a reasonable time has been created. In addition, the number of pending enforcement cases was significantly reduced from 1 855 129 cases at the beginning of 2016 to 712 439 cases at the end of 2018 and 325 648 at the end of 2020.[3] However, many problems remain, and the process of improvement will take time and will require the continuous focus of the Serbian Government.

2.10.3 Transparency of Serbian Jurisprudence

[149] As a general matter, it is not easy to research and identify the jurisprudence of Serbian courts because their judgments are not published in their entirety, nor are they published systematically. For example, Serbian courts in general do not post their rulings on their official websites as is the practice in a number of other countries. Similarly, integral versions of such judgments are not published on the

[2] For more information please, *see* the Annual Report on the Work of the Courts in the Republic of Serbia for 2020 of the Supreme Court of Cassation of 2 Feb. 2021, available at the following link: http://www.vk.sud.rs/sites/default/files/attachments/Annual%20Report%20for%202020_ENG%20FINAL.pdf.

[3] *Ibid.*

relevant professional databases. Instead, only abbreviated or anonymized versions of some of the judgments are made available.

[150] Also, it often happens that when a third party requests a copy of a ruling to be released by the relevant court, the court in question declines to do so on the basis of certain internal rules despite the fact that a general principle of Serbian law guarantees such right in most of the situations. Consequently, in order to get hold of the relevant ruling, the party in question then needs to pursue the official procedure that guarantees access to information of public relevance.

[151] Still, it should be noted that activities on establishing the official central database of the Serbian legal system resulted in introduction of the so-called Legal Information System (in Serbian: *Pravno informacioni sistem; www.pravno-informacioni-sistem.rs*), which is envisaged as a central database for Serbian legislation and court practice. However, this system is still underdeveloped and incomplete and is not publicly available free of charge, so its usefulness is still limited.

2.10.4 Attitude of Serbian Courts Towards Foreigners

[152] Generally speaking, Serbian courts do not seem to favour domestic residents and companies over foreigners. Namely, problems in this context occur due to the lack of experience and sophistication of judicial staff in dealing with more complex issues that typically arise in the context of proceedings with foreign elements.

[153] However, Serbian courts are often perceived as being more lenient towards parties that are economically weaker, such as employees or debtors, and to state-related entities, like public enterprises. This can dramatically jeopardize the interests of creditors, irrespective of whether they are domestic or foreign, and is the prejudice that Serbian courts should be forced to overcome by the proper training and regular internal oversight.

2.10.5 Serbian Arbitral Tribunals

[154] There are two permanent arbitral tribunals in Serbia:

(1) Permanent Court of Arbitration[4] – a permanent arbitration institution organized by the Serbian Chamber of Commerce, a public umbrella chamber of commerce.
(2) Belgrade Arbitration Centre[5] – a permanent arbitration institution organized by the Arbitration Association, a voluntary, non-governmental and non-profit association of legal professionals and other individuals, founded in 2013, which currently comprises over one hundred members – attorneys, university professors and lecturers, judges and commercial lawyers in Serbia with expertise in domestic and international arbitration.

---

[4] http://www.stalnaarbitraza.rs/.

[5] https://www.arbitrationassociation.org/en/about/.

[155] As a general matter, proceedings before arbitral tribunals in Serbia are private and confidential, and the identity of the parties may be revealed only with their approval. Therefore, the decisions of tribunals shall not be published. Instead, only anonymized versions of some of the decisions are made available. In addition to this, the Serbian arbitral tribunals do not provide general information on a number of cases and do not publish jurisprudence. Thus, it is very difficult to track arbitral jurisprudence in Serbia.

3 MERGER CONTROLS. ANTITRUST/ COMPETITION ISSUES

3.1 Relevant Legislation and Competent Authorities

3.1.1 General Remarks

[156] The core rules of Serbian competition law, including merger control, are laid down in the Competition Law, which came into effect in late 2009 and was amended in November 2013. The Competition Law is generally harmonized with the relevant EU competition legal framework (i.e., Council Regulation (EC) No. 139/2004), although the relevant practice is lagging behind the applicable EU standards. The authority in charge of supervising the implementation of the competition law framework in Serbia is the Competition Authority.

3.1.2 Notification Requirements

[157] As to the notification requirements, a transaction must be notified to the Competition Authority if the following two cumulative conditions are satisfied:

(1) the transaction constitutes a concentration; and
(2) at least one of the relevant turnover thresholds is met.

[158] Notwithstanding the above, a concentration made through the takeover of a joint-stock company has to be notified even when the relevant turnover thresholds have not been met.

[159] Pursuant to the Competition Law, until the transaction is approved by the Competition Authority, the concentrating undertakings are prohibited from implementing the transaction. In the event of an ex officio investigation into concentration, the concentrating undertakings are obliged to suspend the implementation of concentration as of the date of receipt by them of the resolution on the initiation of the relevant procedure.

[160] The Competition Law provides that the obligation to suspend the concentration will not generally prevent the execution of a takeover that was duly notified to the competent body in accordance with the applicable rules.

[161] If the Competition Authority discovers that the concentrating undertakings implemented the transaction without filing the necessary notification or prior to the Competition Authority's approval, it is authorized (in addition to imposing the statutory fines) to order the concentrating undertakings to de-merge, that is, to sell the shares, transfer back the business, terminate any relevant agreements and/or adopt other measures necessary to restore effective competition in the relevant market.

3.2 Scope of the Controls

3.2.1 Merger Control Tests

[162] Under the Competition Law, the following transactions constitute concentrations:

- merger and other status changes leading to the acquisition of an undertaking pursuant to the Company Law;
- acquisition by one or more undertakings of direct or indirect control over another undertaking or undertakings; or
- joint venture by two or more undertakings aimed at setting up a new undertaking or acquiring joint control over an existing undertaking that is supposed to perform its operations on a long-term basis and with all the functions of an independent undertaking.

[163] However, the above transactions do not constitute a concentration if they take place between undertakings belonging to the same group (the so-called intra-group exemption). In addition, certain transactions performed by investment entities (e.g., banks, securities brokers and other financial institutions) do not constitute a concentration and thus are not subject to the relevant notification requirement.

[164] Also, two or more concentrations among the same undertakings that are conducted within a period shorter than two years shall be considered one concentration, in which case the effective date of the concentration will be the day on which the last transaction was affected.

[165] Furthermore, a concentration must be notified to the Competition Authority if one of the following two alternative thresholds is met:

(i) the combined aggregate annual turnover of the concentrating undertakings made on the global market in the year preceding the concentration is above EUR100 m, provided that at least one of the undertakings generated turnover on the Serbian market exceeding EUR10 m; or
(ii) the aggregate annual turnover of at least two of the concentrating undertakings on the Serbian market is higher than EUR20 m in the year preceding the concentration, provided that at least two of the concentrating undertakings have an individual annual turnover of more than EUR1 m in the same period on the Serbian market.

[166] Neither the Competition Law nor any of the related regulations provide detailed rules for the calculation of annual turnover for the purposes of the above tests. However, guidelines prescribed by the Competition Authority created sufficient practice to this end.

3.3 Process/Mechanics

3.3.1 Procedure of Notification of Concentration

[167] If a concentration meets one of the two relevant thresholds, it is subject to a notification requirement and the approval of the Competition Authority must be obtained.

[168] The notification of concentration is submitted to the Competition Authority within fifteen days from the date of performing the first of the following acts:

- conclusion of an agreement or contract;
- announcement of a public bid or closing of a public bid; and
- acquisition of control.

3.3.2 Procedure of Notification of Concentration

[169] In the course of the notification procedure, the notifying undertakings must provide the Competition Authority with extensive information on the concentration. The documents and other information which must be provided to the Competition Authority are mainly set out in the relevant decree and are as follows:

(i) name and address of the head office and the business activities of the applicant (i.e., typically presented through an excerpt from the competent register);
(ii) name, address of the head office and the business activities of all concentrating undertakings and market participants referred to in Points (xvii) and (xviii) below (i.e., typically presented through an excerpt from the competent register(s));
(iii) name, address, phone number, fax and e-mail address of an authorized representative or proxy of the applicant, as well as a power of attorney;
(iv) detailed description of the form of concentration;
(v) copy of the agreement or act on the basis of which the concentration is planned or being executed;
(vi) detailed financial statements and other reports showing the financial position of each of the concentrating undertakings for the period of three years preceding the year of the concentration;
(vii) total annual income of the concentrating undertakings, without VAT and other taxes directly related to each of the concentrating undertakings, for the period of three years preceding the year of the concentration (to be submitted separately for each year);

(viii) data on the number of employees for each of the concentrating undertakings for the period of three years preceding the year of the concentration (to be submitted separately for each year);

(ix) list of five major suppliers of relevant products to each of the concentrating undertakings, including the value of supply for the period of three years preceding the year of the concentration (to be submitted separately for each year);

(x) list of five major buyers of relevant products from the concentrating undertakings, including the value of sales, for the period of three years preceding the year of the concentration (to be submitted separately for each year);

(xi) data concerning the value of the product and/or services sales in the relevant market expressed in RSD and the corresponding production volumes expressed in the number of units or relevant measures realized by each of the concentrating undertakings for the period of three years preceding the year of the concentration (to be submitted separately for each year);

(xii) an assessment of the relevant market in which each of the concentrating undertakings and market participants controlled by them or market participants controlling them operate, as well as an assessment of their respective market shares before and after the realization of the concentration;

(xiii) list and assessment of market shares of the main market competitors of the concentrating undertakings in the relevant market;

(xiv) all available analyses, studies, presentations, or any other reports pertaining to the assessment and analysis of the concentration in light of the concentrating undertakings' position in the relevant market, market conditions and the existence of any actual and potential competition in the relevant market;

(xv) organizational chart of the concentrating undertakings and related market participants, particularly providing information on: (a) inter-relations between the concentrating undertakings and related parties; (b) stakes held by controlling parties in the share capital of their subsidiaries; and/or (c) stakes held by subsidiaries in other subsidiaries within the same company group;

(xvi) ownership structure (i.e., before and after the realization of the concentration) over the shares in the concentrating undertakings over which control is acquired;

(xvii) list of other participants in the market in which the concentrating undertakings solely or jointly hold 10% or more shares in the share capital or 10% or more shares carrying voting rights, accompanied by a brief description of the core business activities of such market participants;

(xviii) list of all market participants in which the members of the management or supervisory board of the concentrating undertakings are at the same time the members of the management or supervisory boards, accompanied by a brief description of the core business activities of such market participants;

(xix) decisions of any other relevant authorities related to the concentration or proper evidence that the relevant request has been submitted or is planned to be submitted to such authorities;

(xx) detailed description of the distribution and retail network of goods and/or services in the relevant market, accompanied by a separate description of the distribution and retail network used by the concentrating undertakings;

(xxi) description of the realized or intended research and development investments by the concentrating undertakings (the form and nature of the investment or research, their influence on the production and distribution of the goods and/or services in the relevant market, amount of the proceeds invested or planned to be invested for such purposes, etc.);

(xxii) description and detailed reasons for the implementation of the concentration, that is, the expected benefits for the concentrating undertakings arising from the implementation of the concentration; and

(xxiii) description and detailed explanation of expected benefits for consumers deriving from the implementation of the concentration, including, in particular, information regarding any potential: (a) decrease in prices of goods and/or services; (b) increase in quality of goods and services; (c) introduction of innovations; (d) increase in the available selection and/or range of goods and/or services for consumers.

[170] Apart from the information and documents listed above, the applicant may submit other data and supporting documentation that it considers relevant for the assessment of the intended concentration.

[171] If requested, the applicant is also obliged to submit additional data which the Competition Authority considers relevant for the assessment of the intended concentration.

3.3.3 Proceedings

[172]

(i) Phase I Proceeding.
If, based on the submitted evidence and other facts known to the Competition Authority, it is clear that the concentration is not prohibited by the Competition Law, the Competition Authority will approve the concentration in the so-called phase I proceeding which lasts for up to one month.

If the Competition Authority fails to issue a decision after the expiry of this period of time, the transaction is deemed to be approved.

However, the statutory period of time allocated for summary proceedings is automatically suspended whenever the Competition Authority requests additional information on the concentration. In other words, requests for additional information/documents automatically extend the process and the aforementioned period of time does not continue to run until the requested information/documents are provided to the Competition Authority.

Please note that within the phase I proceeding, a simplified procedure may be applied in situations where notified concentration does not raise any substantive doubts, provided that the concentration falls under a certain category.

The Competition Authority shall apply the simplified procedure to the following categories of concentrations:

- two or more undertakings merge, or one or more undertakings acquire sole or joint control of another undertaking, provided that none of the parties to the concentration is engaged in business activities in the same product and geographical market or in a product market that is upstream or downstream from a product market in which any other party to the concentration is engaged;
- two or more undertakings merge, or one or more undertakings acquire sole or joint control of another undertaking and: (i) two or more of the parties to the concentration are engaged in business activities in the same product and geographical market (horizontal relationships), provided that their combined market share is less than 20%; or (ii) one or more of the parties to the concentration is engaged in business activities in a product market that is upstream or downstream from a product market in which any other party to the concentration is engaged (vertical relationships), provided that none of their individual or combined market shares exceeds 30%;
- a party is to acquire sole control of an undertaking over which it already has joint control; or
- if the combined market share of all the parties to the concentration that is in a horizontal relationship is less than 40%, provided that the Herfindahl-Hirschman Index (HHI) delta resulting from the concentration is less than 150.

It can normally be expected that concentrations falling within one of the above categories will not raise serious doubts as to their compatibility with the relevant market. Consequently, the simplified procedure requires the applicant to provide the Competition Authority with less information and documentation in comparison to the regular phase I notification proceeding. For example, under the simplified procedure, financial statements and the list of the top-five suppliers/customers should be provided for the year preceding the year in which concentration is to be notified, while under the regular notification procedure, such documents should be provided for three years preceding the year in which the concentration is to be notified. In addition, in the case of the simplified procedure, some information/documents are not required (e.g., details regarding planned entrances into and exits from the relevant market).

However, if there are circumstances that indicate that the concentration might not be approved, the applicant should submit to the Competition Authority all the evidence that is required for an ordinary notification. Such circumstances exist particularly in cases where there is no established case practice to determine the relevant market, in emerging markets where a party is a new or potential entrant, or where the relevant market is highly concentrated, etc.

(ii) Ex Officio Proceeding.
After gaining knowledge of an implemented concentration that was not notified to the Competition Authority, or in case of more complicated concentrations, the latter may conduct an investigation into such concentration, provided: (i) that the mutual market share of the concentrating undertakings on the Serbian market is at least 40%; (ii) that the Competition Authority has grounds to assume that the relevant concentration does not comply with the conditions prescribed by the Competition Law; or (iii) in any other case of concentration that was not approved when it was subject to prior approval in accordance with the Competition Law.
The Competition Authority is obliged to reach a decision in this type of investigation within a period of four months but the same potential delays relating to potential requests for additional information apply. If the Competition Authority fails to issue a decision after the expiry of this four-month period, the transaction is deemed to be approved.

3.3.4 Timing Implications

[173] The Competition Authority is generally known to follow the statutory deadline when rendering relevant decisions, especially in the context of the summary proceeding. As the whole process before the Competition Authority is quite bureaucratic, the undertaking entities are typically represented by local legal advisors. In the course of either of the proceedings, legal advisors often contact the Competition Authority staff directly to obtain their informal views on the application status, potential deficiencies and means to cure such issues, and other related matters. The Competition Authority staff is generally professional, friendly and forthcoming and is also often ready to accommodate requests for formal meetings in the course of which some more complex issues can be discussed with them.

3.3.5 Competition Authority Practice

[174] Since the Serbian competition law practice is catching up with EU standards, and due to the fact that the Serbian market is a relatively small one on which complicated mergers have not been so common, at least up until now, a very large percentage of filings have been cleared in the course of summary proceedings. Only a few concentrations have been rejected and/or conditionally approved by the Competition Authority, primarily due to the latter's view that they would result in the creation of a dominant position (e.g., Sunoko *Case*).

[175] To the best of our knowledge, the views of trade competitors are not usually taken into account when assessing relevant merger filing notifications. However, historically, the Competition Authority launched a few investigations with respect to the abuse of dominant position by taking into account the views and information obtained from or provided by the competitors of the relevant company that was being investigated. For example, in the Frikom *Case*, which concerned the market for ice creams in Serbia, Nestle provided information to the Competition Authority about the alleged abuse of dominant position by a regional ice cream producer, Frikom. Additionally, for the first time in July 2015, the Competition Authority conducted dawn raids with respect to the distribution of electronic cigarettes and liquid for electronic cigarettes. Proceedings were initiated on the ground of suspicion that the undertakings concluded agreements on setting minimum prices in retail trade. Since that time, the Competition Authority has started to be more active in this field and conducted more dawn raids:

(i) Remedies.
The scope for offering remedies in order to obtain clearance is mostly related to structural and behavioural measures. The structural measures usually comprise divestment of certain assets within the relevant deadline set by the Competition Authority. In addition to this, prohibition to acquire such assets within a certain period of time in future (e.g., ten years) may also be imposed on the relevant company.
As to the behavioural measures, in the practice of the Competition Authority to date, they are usually related to the obligation of the relevant company to submit monthly or semi-annual reports to the Competition Authority which will contain figures about sales as well as information about the prices for the relevant products of such company. If prices are to be changed, then the relevant company is obliged to provide further explanations about reasons for such changes and such reasons are evaluated by the Competition Authority.

(ii) Remedial Measures.
The Competition Authority may, in addition to fines (*see* paragraph **[175]** (v) below), impose remedial measures to be taken by the concentrating undertakings, such as ordering them to de-merge or to adopt other measures necessary to restore the conditions existing before the implementation of concentration on the relevant market.

(iii) The Timing of Approvals in the Context of a Bid for a Publicly Held Company.
The relevant need to obtain a concentration approval in the context of acquisition of public companies should be duly taken into consideration in advance of each such transaction and the relevant period of time within which the Competition Authority is expected to render its approval should be factored into the overall timing in each case. It should also be examined whether approvals by some other regulatory bodies (e.g., NBS in the case of banks and insurance companies) should also be sought.

(iv) Sanctions.
Sanctions for potential breach of the merger control or other antitrust rules in Serbia include fines and remedial actions. In addition to this, for the abuse of the dominant position, a responsible person within the company may be sentenced to imprisonment in the range between six months and five years and also with a monetary fine.

(v) Fines.

The Competition Authority may impose severe fines for breaches of the relevant rules. These fines may amount:

- to up to 10% of the net turnover achieved by the relevant undertaking and/or company group on the Serbian market in the preceding financial year in the event of a breach of the prohibition on the implementation of the transaction without approval or the implementation of the concentration before the approval of the Competition Authority has been granted, or for non-compliance with the Competition Authority's order to de-merge;
- to between EUR500 and EUR5 000 per day for: (a) failing to comply with an enforceable decision of the Competition Authority; (b) failing to submit information requested by the Competition Authority within the required period and/or submitting incorrect, incomplete or false information; and (c) not notifying a concentration within the timeframe prescribed by the Competition Law.

In any event, the fines for procedural breaches may not exceed an amount equal to 10% of the total annual turnover achieved by the relevant undertaking and/or company group calculated pursuant to the Competition Law.

3.4 Anticompetitive Restraints

3.4.1 General Remarks

[176] The Competition Law does not regulate limitations on the permissible duration and/or geographical scope of competition restraints related to the key employees of a business that is being sold. However, the Labour Law provides that such competition restrictions may not last longer than two years. Pursuant to the applicable rules and practice, the employee in question is entitled to compensation throughout the relevant period of time through which the relevant restrictions are set to apply.

[177] In the event that the relevant post-acquisition situation requires that the management team and other key employees of the target are incentivized to remain with the relevant company, certain measures such as cash and/or share bonus schemes may be offered to them. Also, in the event any of such key persons are also former shareholders of the target, an option is to structure their compensation for the shares they sold to the acquirer on an earn-out basis, thus motivating them to remain with the target and increase its profits for several years following the acquisition.

[178] The main constraints affecting competition in Serbia are horizontal and vertical restrictive agreements and abuse of dominant position.

3.4.2 Individual and Block Exemptions Rules

[179] In general, restrictive agreements may be exempted if they stimulate technical or economic development and relevant customers may benefit from such arrangements, provided that other market participants are not limited by them and/or that competition has not been excluded from the relevant market.

[180] Contrary to the current practice in a number of other jurisdictions, the Competition Authority may exempt individual restrictive agreements for a period which cannot exceed eight years based on a request by the relevant party to such restrictive agreement. Such party has a burden of proof that the relevant restrictive agreement shall contribute to the technical and economic development and shall not restrict the competition on the relevant market. The Competition Authority is obliged to issue a decision on the individual exemption within sixty days from the day of filing of the relevant request.

[181] In March 2010, the Serbian Government enacted block exemption regulations for vertical and horizontal agreements. For a block exemption to be applied in the case of a vertical agreement, the market share of each of the parties to such agreement cannot be higher than 25%. For horizontal agreements, if the market share of all parties to such agreement at the moment of conclusion of such agreement is not more than 20% and subsequently increases but in any case does not exceed a 25% market share, the exemption is applied for a period of two consecutive years following the year in which the market share surpassed 20% for the first time. In addition to this, if the market share of all parties to a horizontal agreement at the moment of conclusion of such agreement is not more than 20% and subsequently increases above 25% but below 30%, the exemption applies within the period of six months following the period in which the market share was increased above 25% for the first time.

3.4.3 Agreements of Minor Importance

[182] Agreements of minor importance are the agreements between market participants whose aggregate market share on the relevant market in Serbia is not higher than: (i) 10% in case of horizontal agreements; (ii) 15% in the case of vertical agreements; (iii) 10% if the relevant agreement has characteristics of both horizontal and vertical agreements and it is difficult to assess which of them prevail; and (iv) 30% if the relevant agreement has been concluded between different market participants, none of whom has individually more than 5% market share on each relevant market on which the effects of such agreement have been manifested.

[183] In principle, agreements of minor importance are allowed, unless they are the so-called hard-core agreements, whose objective is price-fixing, restriction of production or sale (i.e., in case of horizontal agreements), or division of the relevant market (i.e., in case of vertical agreements).

3.4.4 Competition Authority

[184] The Competition Authority is the sole regulatory and administrative authority in charge of the implementation of the competition law framework and renders all the relevant decisions related to the competition law matters. A decision of the Competition Authority may be appealed to the Serbian Administrative Court within thirty days of the delivery of the relevant decision to the party in question. Such an appeals process does not automatically suspend the implementation of the Competition Authority's decision. However, the Competition Authority has a right to postpone the enforceability of the decision if such enforcement would cause serious damage to the relevant party.

4 TAXATION ASPECTS

4.1 Nature of the Tax Regime and Specific Taxes

[185] Tax jurisdiction in Serbia is deemed as a certain tax environment and as an opaque system. Tax rules are generally considered to be simple and are aggressively enforced by the Tax Authority. In practice, the Ministry of Finance interprets tax legislation by issuing rulings for each specific matter upon the request of taxpayers, which rulings are obligatory for the Tax Authority.

4.2 Liability for Tax

4.2.1 Corporate Income Tax

[186] Corporate income tax is set at a flat rate of 15%.

[187] Resident companies, as well as non-resident companies, provided that they have a permanent establishment in Serbia, are liable to pay corporate income tax on profits generated. Resident companies are deemed to be those registered in Serbia or having their effective management/control in Serbia. Resident companies are taxed on their worldwide income and non-resident companies on income generated through their permanent establishments/branch in Serbia.

[188] The basis for taxation is taxable profits of the company, i.e., profits declared in the Profit & Loss account, adjusted in accordance with the Corporate Income Tax Law provisions.

[189] The Financial/fiscal year of a taxpayer in Serbia is generally set as a calendar year. Alternatively, the financial/fiscal year may differ from a calendar year (any twelve-month period), subject to pre-approval of the Ministry of Finance/NBS and provided that certain conditions are met.

[190] A taxpayer that invests more than RSD1 bn (approximately EUR8.5 m) in its fixed assets, which are used for its main business activity, and, within the investment

period, engages at least one hundred new employees for an indefinite period of time, shall be exempted from the corporate income tax liability for a period of ten years in proportion to the amount of the investment.

4.2.2 Capital Gain Tax

[191] Capital gain tax is set at a 15% flat rate.

[192] Resident companies, as well as non-resident companies, are liable for this tax provided that they have permanent establishments in Serbia. Capital gain shall be deemed to exist in case of income generated from sale (or other transfer for consideration) of:

- an immovable property which had been used for the business activity of the seller prior to the sale (recognized as a fixed asset in the seller's books);
- IP rights;
- a share in capital of a legal entity, stocks and other securities recognized in the accounting as long-term financial investments;
- an investment unit acquired from the open investment fund in accordance with relevant legislation; and
- digital assets, unless the taxpayer has a license to provide services related to digital assets and acquired digital assets exclusively for resale within the provision of services related to digital assets.

[193] Additionally, capital gains are also deemed to exist for income generated by a non-resident from sale of assets described in paragraph **[192]** above (except for sale of IP rights), but also from the sale of an immovable property located in Serbia and not used for business activity of the seller prior to the sale.

[194] The capital gain tax base is the difference between the sales price and purchase price determined in accordance with the Corporate Income Tax Law. If the difference is negative, a capital loss will arise. Capital losses can be carried forward for five years and used to offset future years' capital gains (if any).

4.2.3 VAT

[195] The standard VAT rate is set at 20%.

[196] A reduced VAT rate is set at 10% and applies to the supply of basic food items such as bread, milk, flour, cooking oil, fresh and frozen fruits, vegetables, meat, fish and eggs, but also to listed drugs, agricultural fertilizers, pesticides, textbooks, daily newspapers, hotel services, natural gas, first transfer of ownership on residential buildings, etc.

[197] A separate VAT regime applies to supplies made by farmers. Namely, farmers are entitled to 8% VAT remuneration on supplies they make, which is payable by buyers-legal entities and charged on the reverse-charge mechanism.

[198] In addition to the above, certain supplies are zero-rated (i.e., exempt from VAT with the right to recover input VAT) such as export, transport services related to import and export, entry of goods into a free trade zone, supplies to embassies and diplomatic bodies, supplies made in accordance with donation agreements, loan and international agreements concluded by the state, etc. In general, financial, banking and insurance services are deemed exempt from VAT without input VAT recovery rights.

[199] As a general rule, the following is subject to VAT:

- supply of goods and services made by a taxpayer in the territory of Serbia for consideration within the taxpayer's business activity;
- importation of goods in Serbia.

[200] The place of supply of goods is by general rule considered to be the place where the goods are located at the time of dispatch or transport to the purchaser. If the goods are delivered without dispatch or transport, it is the place where the goods are situated at the moment of delivery. As for the place of supply of services, the general rule is:

- if a service is provided to a taxpayer (B2B – business-to-business-rule), the place of supply of such service shall be the place where the service recipient has its head office or a permanent establishment;
- if a service is provided to a person who is not a taxpayer (B2C – business-to-customer rule), the place of supply shall be the place where the service provider has its head office or a permanent establishment.

When a service is provided by a taxpayer in Serbia, for the purpose of applying the rules for determining the place of supply of service, the following entities are considered to be the taxpayers to whom the service is provided (B2B rule):

- any person who carries out the business as a permanent activity;
- legal entities, state authorities and local government bodies in Serbia;
- foreign legal entities, state authorities and local government bodies registered for payment of taxes on consumption in the country in which they have the head office.

[201] Separate VAT rules apply to the construction business, the supply of secondary raw materials and the first transfer of ownership over newly constructed real estate, where VAT is generally charged by the supply/service recipient on the basis of a reverse-charge mechanism (subject to certain pre-conditions).

[202] Mandatory VAT registration applies to each entity whose:

- turnover exceeds RSD8 m (approximately EUR68 300) in any previous twelve months; or
- forecasted turnover for the following twelve months is higher than RSD8 m at the moment of commencing business operations in Serbia.

[203] An entity whose turnover does not exceed RSD8 m in a twelve-month period can opt for voluntary VAT registration at any time during the year.

[204] A foreign person is required to appoint a VAT proxy for each supply of goods and/or services that is carried out on the territory of Serbia in accordance with the place of supply rules envisaged by the Serbian VAT Law. However, a foreign person is not required to appoint a VAT proxy and register for VAT in Serbia in the following situations (exceptions to the general rule):

- if supply is carried out exclusively to customers in Serbia who are VAT payers;
- if supply is carried out to entities referred to in Article 9, paragraph 1 of the VAT Law as follows: the Republic of Serbia and its bodies, territorial autonomy and local self-government bodies, legal entities established by law or by an act of a Republic of Serbia's body, or by territorial autonomy and local self-government bodies in order to conduct state administration or local self-government;
- in case of providing transport of passengers service by buses for which the VAT base is determined as an average transportation fee for each transport;
- if providing VAT-exempt supplies in accordance with the VAT Law (with or without the right to deduct input VAT).

The obligation of a foreign entity to appoint a VAT proxy and register for VAT in Serbia does not depend on volume of supply made by a foreign person in a particular period, nor is relevant the number of transactions carried out by a foreign entity in a particular period (one-off transaction versus several transactions) on the territory of Serbia.

VAT proxy of a foreign person is jointly and severally liable for VAT obligations of the foreign person.

[205] VAT return is submitted quarterly by entities generating turnover below RSD50 m (approximately EUR427 300) in a twelve-month period. Newly established entities and entities having a turnover in a twelve-month period above the RSD50 m threshold are obliged to submit VAT returns monthly. The submission date is the fifteenth of the month for the previous month for both monthly and quarterly taxpayers.

4.2.4 Property Transfer Tax

[206] The property transfer rate is set at the rate of 2.5%.

[207] The tax applies on transfers with consideration (and provided that they are not subject to VAT) on:

- ownership over immovable property;
- IP rights;
- ownership of overused motor vehicles, vessels and aircraft (certain exceptions apply);
- rights of use over construction land; and
- rent of construction land in public ownership for a period longer than one year or for an indefinite time period for the purpose of erecting buildings.

[208] The basis for taxation is set as the agreed sale/lease/use price, which may be reassessed by the Tax Authorities if it falls below the market value within sixty days from the date of submitting the transfer tax return.

4.2.5 Property Tax

[209] Companies pay property tax at the rate of up to 0.4% (the exact rate is determined by each local municipality).

[210] The following is subject to property tax:

- ownership right over immovable property (buildings and land larger than ten acres);
- tenancy right, determined for the benefit of a natural person;
- construction land usage right larger than ten acres in area;
- usage right and usage of state-owned immovable property (in accordance with the public property legislation) by the holder of the right of use;
- use of real estate in public ownership by real estate users in accordance with the law governing public property;
- occupancy of immovable for which owner is unknown or undetermined;
- occupancy of the state-owned immovable property without legal ground (*sine causa* occupancy); and
- occupancy and usage of immovable property based on financial leasing agreement.

[211] Tax liability is determined annually by submitting tax return by 31 March of the current year (31 January for natural persons) on the basis of average square meter price in the zone where specific immovable property is located (published by local authority) and actual surface of the immovable property in question. Certain exceptions to this general rule apply, e.g., the tax base for certain immovable property is the net book value of the asset in accounting records as of 31 December of the previous year.

[212] Taxpayers who keep their own business records apply a self-taxation method in the determination and payment of the property tax, while taxpayers who do not keep business records pay taxes according to the assessment issued by their tax authorities' office.

[213] As an exception from the above general rule, in the determination of tax base of an immovable property recorded in the books in accordance with the fair value model, the net book value of the asset in question as of 31 December of the prior year will be regarded as the relevant tax base.

4.2.6 Municipality Taxes

[214] Municipality taxes are paid for displaying a company's name on the business premises, keeping motor vehicles and keeping gaming machines and devices. The rates depend on the size of the company in accordance with applicable accounting standards, the main business activity of the company, and the city zone in which the activity is conducted.

[215] The eco-tax is not only paid for products that after use become special waste but also for the packaging in which the product is packaged. The regular deadline for submitting the annual report on products that set up special waste after use is

31 March 2021 – the report is submitted twice: electronically and in a printed form by post. The eco-tax is mandatory for all businessmen who import or produce certain products that set up special waste streams after use. The report is submitted to the Environmental Protection Agency in the current year for products that are enlarged or manufactured during the preceding year.

4.2.7 Social Insurance

[216] Mandatory social security contributions are prescribed for health insurance, pension and disability insurance and unemployment insurance.

[217] The applicable social security contribution rates are starting from 1 January 2023:

- pension and disability insurance – 14% for an employer and 10% for an employee;
- health insurance – 5.15% payable by both an employer and an employee; and
- unemployment insurance – 0.75% payable by the employee only.

[218] The minimal and maximal social security contribution base applies to salary payment. The minimal monthly base is set at 35% of the average monthly salary paid in Serbia for the period of previous twelve months starting from September in the current year, as per official statistics. The maximum monthly base is set at five times the average salary paid in Serbia for the period of previous twelve months starting from September in the current year, as per official statistics.

[219] Foreign natural persons assigned to work in Serbia may apply for an exemption from the mandatory social security contribution liability in Serbia, provided that the social security convention applies between Serbia and the relevant person's country of employment (subject to the fulfilment of the conditions envisaged by the relevant convention).

4.2.8 Excises

[220] Producers and importers of the following goods in Serbia are liable for excise duty on the following:

- oil derivatives;
- biofuel and bioliquids;
- tobacco products, including tobacco products that are heated but do not burn during use;
- nicotine bags;
- alcohol beverages;
- coffee;
- liquid filling for electronic cigarettes;
- electricity for final consumption;
- natural gas for final consumption.

[221] The excise duty is set as specific (oil derivate, biofuel and bioliquids, alcohol beverages, coffee, tobacco, liquid filling of electronic cigarettes) and combined specific and ad valorem to the retail price (cigarettes and electricity for final consumption). An ad valorem duty is set as a percentage of the value of an item, unlike a specific duty that is a fixed sum imposed on each item of a kind, regardless of their individual values.

[222] The rates of the excise duty are adjusted on an annual basis, while the minimum excise duty for tobacco products is adjusted on a semi-annual basis.

4.2.9 Customs

[223] The customs rates for imported goods are provided in the Customs Tariff and are applied on goods that originate from countries with which Serbia has a most-favoured-nation clause trading status or if this clause is applied to goods originating from Serbia. On goods originating from countries with which Serbia has concluded a free trade agreement, the rates provided in that agreement will apply. On goods imported from other countries, Customs Tariff rates increased by 70% shall apply.

4.2.10 Capital Duty or Other Duties on Share Capital

[224] There are no capital duties or other duties on share capital in Serbia, apart from minor fees for registration purposes.

4.2.11 Capital Allowances

[225] There are no specific rules on capital allowance or deductions or other deductions in respect of capital expenditure.

4.2.12 Tax Consolidation: Group Relief of Gains and Losses

[226] Gains or losses cannot be transferred from one company to another within a group of companies unless they apply for tax consolidation. This rule applies to both operating and capital gains or losses.

[227] Only resident companies may apply for tax consolidation, provided that the resident parent company owns at least a 75% share in its resident subsidiaries. The consolidation is subject to pre-approval by the local tax authorities' office and, once approved, applies for at least five years.

[228] Dividends from the foreign subsidiary are included in the parent company's taxable income, but the parent company can claim credit on taxes paid abroad on such income. The right to a tax credit can be exercised only if the parent company held at least 10% of the foreign subsidiary's shares for at least twelve months before the date of the distribution.

4.3 Tax Considerations Arising on M&A Transactions

4.3.1 Sale of Shares

[229] In the case of the sale of shares, a vendor, who is a natural person, will have to consider his/her capital gains tax obligation. Namely, the positive difference between sale and purchase price of shares is subject to capital gains tax at the rate of 15%. No other taxes (transfer tax, VAT, etc.) would be due.

[230] A vendor in the form of a limited company/a joint-stock company will also have to consider its capital gains tax obligation. Namely, the positive difference between sale and purchase price of shares is subject to capital gains tax also at the rate of 15%. Capital gains are taxed separately from operating profits. No other taxes (transfer tax, VAT, etc.) would be due. Exception is prescribed for capital gains on the basis of the copyright or related right on the deposited copyright work and rights in connection with the invention that implies that only 20% of the capital gains are taxed.

[231] The purchaser, both as a natural person and in the form of a limited company/joint-stock company, will have no tax liabilities.

4.3.2 Sale of Assets

[232] As for the sale of assets, the vendor, both as a natural person and in the form of a limited liability company, will have to consider its capital gain tax obligation if the transfer of particular assets is subject to capital gain tax.

[233] From the perspective of the vendor, the sale of assets may trigger VAT. The sale of certain assets or assets forming a business unit can qualify as being outside of the scope of VAT, but this has to be assessed in each particular situation. The standard VAT rate in Serbia is 20%.

[234] The purchaser and the vendor, both as a natural person and in the form of a legal entity, will also have to consider the transfer tax implications. The transfer tax is due on the transfer (with consideration) of certain assets (i.e., immovable property, IP rights, motor vehicles, vessels and aircraft, use of construction land). The relevant tax rate is 2.5%. It is the vendor who is responsible for the transfer tax. However, if the vendor does not pay tax, that triggers the liability of the purchaser, who could be either jointly and severally or secondarily liable.

[235] If the parties are independent in negotiating value, one of the exemptions can be a transaction between related entities when transfer pricing rules need to be observed.

[236] The postponement of capital gain tax occurs in all changes of status under the Company Law (i.e., mergers, de-mergers and spin-offs). Capital gain tax is postponed until the moment when the acquirer disposes of the particular asset. Advance tax clearance does not exist in Serbia.

[237] Operating losses can be carried forward for five years but can be used solely by the company that made the losses. More precisely, losses cannot be made available to other group members (unless tax consolidation is approved). However, in case of changes of status under the Company Law, losses can be transferred to an acquirer who is a legal successor.

[238] Deferred payments, retentions, holdbacks and 'earn-outs' are not commonly used in order to achieve an advantageous tax treatment.

[239] Acquisition expenses are generally deductible as a business expense.

4.4 Structuring the Investment: Withholding Taxes

4.4.1 Subjected Payments and Tax Rates

[240] The standard withholding tax rate for legal entities is set at 20% and is applied unless otherwise provided in a double tax treaty that Serbia has in place. The following payments to non-residents are subject to withholding tax:

(i) Dividends.
Dividends paid to foreign individual shareholders, who are natural persons, are charged at a 15% tax rate. Dividends from the foreign subsidiary are included in the parent company's taxable income, but the parent company can claim credit on taxes paid abroad on such income. The right to tax credit can be exercised only if the parent company held at least 10% of the foreign subsidiary's shares for at least twelve months before the date of the distribution.

(ii) Interest.
Interest paid to foreign corporate/group shareholders or affiliates is subject to withholding tax at the rate of 20%. Interest paid out to a company in a jurisdiction with a preferential tax regime is subject to a 25% withholding tax. A tax credit is available for interest received from foreign corporate/group shareholders or affiliates.

(iii) *IP*
IP royalties paid to foreign corporate/group shareholders or affiliates are subject to withholding tax at the rate of 20%. If paid out to a company in a jurisdiction with a preferential tax regime, IP royalty is subject to a 25% withholding tax. A tax credit is available for IP royalties received from foreign corporate/group shareholders or affiliates.

(iv) Lease of Immovable and Movable Property.
Rent fees paid to non-residents for both movable goods and immovable property are subject to withholding tax at the rate of 20%. If paid out to a company in a jurisdiction with a preferential tax regime, the fees are subject to a 25% withholding tax.

(v) Service Fees for market research, accounting and auditing, and other legal and business consulting services.

Service fees payable to a non-resident company are subject to withholding tax at the standard rate of 20% for services such as market research services, accounting and audit services, and other legal and business consulting services. However, if the fees are paid out to a company in a jurisdiction with a preferential tax regime, then withholding tax at the rate of 25% becomes due.

4.4.2 Double Tax Treaties

[241] As of 1 January 2023, Serbia has sixty-four effective double tax treaties. The general conditions for the application of a double tax treaty are as follows:

- a certificate of residence of the recipient of income needs to be presented to the Serbian payer; and
- the non-resident income recipient should be able to prove that it is the beneficial owner of the income.

4.5 Debt Financing

[242] The finance costs for acquisitions are deductible under the general rules valid for the deductibility of finance costs.

4.6 Thin Capitalization

[243] Thin capitalization rules apply to interest on loans charged between parties. However, if a loan is granted by a related party, both the debt-to-equity ratio and market interest rate should be considered, i.e., related party interest is subject to the following two tests.

4.6.1 Thin Capitalization Test

[244] The debt-to-equity ratio is set at 4:1. Interest that exceeds this ratio is regarded as non-deductible for tax purposes (for banks and leasing companies, a 10:1 ratio applies).

4.6.2 Transfer Pricing Test

[245] Interest that does not exceed the debt-to-equity ratio (interest expenses recognized as tax-deductible in the above step) is subject to the transfer pricing test. For the purposes of determining the amount of interest that would be regarded as an 'arm's length' interest, the Corporate Income Tax Law provides for the following two alternative approaches:

(1) interest to be compared with interest rate prescribed annually by the Ministry of Finance; or
(2) interest to be supported as an 'arm's length' interest by applying general transfer pricing methods.

[246] Exceeding amount of interest is regarded as non-deductible for tax purposes.

4.7 Transfer Pricing

[247] All companies having transactions with both resident and non-resident-related parties in a fiscal year are obliged to prepare and submit to the tax authorities in Serbia their transfer pricing documentation files.

[248] An entity is deemed as a related party if it has the possibility of control or considerable influence on the business decisions made. Effectively, this means either ownership of at least 25% of the shares or possession of at least 25% of the voting rights in the managing body of the entity.

[249] Tax legislation envisages that the transfer pricing documentation is to be submitted to the tax authorities together with the corporate income tax calculation, i.e., within 180 days from the last date of a tax period. Transfer pricing documentation file should be either prepared in Serbian language or officially translated in Serbian.

[250] The following mandatory elements of each transfer pricing study are prescribed by the Transfer Pricing Rulebook:

- analysis of the group of related entities whose member is the taxpayer;
- business activity analysis;
- functional analysis;
- selection of transfer pricing method used in the determination of transfer pricing;
- conclusion – is it required to amend taxable base for related party transactions;
- appendices – review of data used by the taxpayer in the determination of 'arm's-length' prices.

[251] In general, local transfer pricing legislation recognizes and follows the Organisation for Economic Co-operation and Development (OECD) Transfer Pricing Guidelines. Consequently, one of the following methods can be used in determining transfer prices according to the 'arm's-length' principle:

- Comparable Uncontrolled Price (CUP) Method.
- Resale Price Method.
- Cost Plus Method.
- Transactional Net Margin Method (TNMM).
- Profit Split Method.

[252] None of the above methods is preferred. This implies that taxpayers are allowed to choose methods to be used in the determination of 'arm's-length' prices and preparation of transfer pricing documentation.

[253] The method is chosen on the level of each type of transaction. Combining two or more methods is also allowed. However, the one that has been chosen must be practically applicable and should eventually result in a reasonable estimate of effects in accordance with the 'arm's-length' principle.

[254] In documenting transfer prices, certain simplifications apply in case one of the following two conditions was met:

(1) specific related party transaction is regarded to be a one-off transaction and does not exceed RSD8 m in total in a fiscal year (approximately EUR68 000); or
(2) the value of all transactions with a specific related party during a fiscal year does not exceed RSD8 m (approximately EUR68 000) in total.

[255] If one of the above conditions is met, taxpayers are allowed to submit a simplified transfer pricing documentation file without detailed analysis and without supporting the 'arm's-length' approach.

[256] From 9 October 2021, the amended Transfer Pricing Rulebook comes into force, setting out the new rules on the annual report on controlled transactions of the international group of related parties (Country-by-Country (CbC) Report).

[257] The obligation to submit the annual report lies with a resident taxpayer who is considered the ultimate owner legal entity of an international group of related legal entities whose total consolidated income in the previous year amounted to at least EUR750 m. The annual report is submitted on the CbC form in paper form no later than twelve months from the end of the tax period.

[258] The amendments did not define a separate notification on the submitter of the annual report, but the taxpayer is obliged to provide the following information in the annual documentation on transfer prices:

- is the taxpayer a member of an international group of related parties; and
- is it considered the ultimate owner in terms of Article 61v of the Corporate Income Tax Law which regulates the submission of the annual report.

If the ultimate owner is not considered, information on the identity and residency of the ultimate owner should be provided.

5 EMPLOYMENT CONSIDERATIONS

5.1 Legislative Framework

[259] The main legislative framework affecting labour and employment in Serbia is set out in the Labour Law, which underwent comprehensive and substantive

revisions in July 2014. These amendments to the Labour Law have certainly contributed to the creation of a more favourable business environment, as most of the changes were employer-friendly and intended to reduce the overall cost of labour.

[260] In addition to the Labour Law, the following laws represent additional sources of important rules in the area of labour and employment: (i) the Law on Protection of the Security and Health at Work; (ii) the Law on Strike; (iii) the Law on Employment and Insurance in Case of Unemployment; (iv) the Law on Employing of Foreigners; and (v) the newly introduced Agency Employment Law. The latter was adopted in late 2019 and it regulates the rights and obligations of employees who conclude an employment contract with a temporary employment agency in order to be temporarily transferred to the beneficiary employer. This law provides equal treatment of assigned employees in terms of exercising certain employment rights and employment conditions, the manner and conditions of assignment of employees, the relationship between the agency and the beneficiary's employer and the obligations of the agency and the beneficiary's employer towards the assigned employees.

5.2 Employment Protection

5.2.1 General Remarks

[261] When it comes to the issue of transfer of employees in the context of business transfers, the Transfers of Undertakings Directive 2001/23/EC (*TUPE Directive*) has not been fully reflected in the Serbian Labour Law. This is in spite of the general proclamation by the Serbian Government that the implementation of the TUPE Directive was one of the objectives behind the original adoption of the Labour Law back in 2005.

[262] Pursuant to Articles 147–151 of the Serbian Labour Law, in case of corporate status changes (e.g., merger, spin-off) or 'change of employer', the collective bargaining agreement and all employment contracts shall automatically be transferred to the succeeding employer. However, these provisions are rather unclear, since they do not define what is meant by the 'change of employer' and whether this refers to all types of transfers of undertakings or businesses, in the sense of the TUPE Directive, or is meant to be limited to only some of the scenarios available in practice. The respective provisions of the Labour Law also fail to even mention the term 'transfer of an undertaking or a business' and the current lack of any court practice on this issue leaves a wide space for various interpretations, which are mostly completely opposite to the objectives and concepts of the TUPE Directive. In light of the foregoing, it is, for example, not clear whether there should be an automatic transfer of employment contracts in case of transfer of a business by way of an asset deal.

[263] Since the commencement of the economic transition in Serbia, the representation of employees in companies' management has been practically completely excluded. Formally, there is no obligation under the applicable framework in Serbia that employees should be represented in various corporate management bodies.

5.2.2 Obligation of Information or Consultation with Respect to the Transfer of Shares or the Sale of a Business

[264] The mentioned amendments to the Labour Law excluded a need to prepare a notification to employees in the context of change of the employer's ownership by means of a share deal. However, in case of corporate status changes (e.g., merger, spin-off), the employer is obliged to notify the representative trade union or, if there is no such trade union, all the company employees about:

- agreed or proposed date of the planned status change;
- reasons for such change; and/or
- legal, economic and social consequences of the change and potential measures that need to be taken for mitigation of these consequences.

[265] The relevant notification should be made at least fifteen days before the relevant changes are supposed to take place.

[266] The above requirements also apply in the context of the so-called change of employer although, as already noted above, it is not clear what type of situation this represents in practice and whether it, for example, covers asset deals.

[267] The relevant rules do not prescribe any direct legal consequences for violation of the above duty to inform, but only for violating the acquired rights of the employees after the transfer.

[268] The Labour Law provides that if an employee refuses to accept to be transferred to another employer due to a corporate status change or 'change of employer', the original employer would be authorized to dismiss the employee without any statutory severance payment.

5.2.3 Works Councils/Trade Unions Rights

[269] Although legal possibility to establish work councils is envisaged under the Labour Law, they have not been formed in practice. However, trade unions do exist in Serbia but their influence is currently quite weak and they do not represent a strong force in the process of achievement of employee rights. At the moment, the strongest trade unions exist within the companies which had been historically state-owned and which were privatized in the course of the privatization process. Certain special rights are granted or recognized to trade unions and their representatives, such as protection from termination of employment, a certain amount of paid annual leave in order to perform various activities related to the trade union work, and usage of premises belonging to the employer for the purpose of trade union activities.

[270] As already noted above, employees are supposed to be notified about, among others, the planned status changes involving the employer, but they cannot block such transactions.

[271] As to mass redundancies, an employer is obliged to undertake, in cooperation with, *inter alia*, the employee representatives, measures which could avoid a mass dismissal with the aim of placing relevant redundant employees in any of the employer's other workplaces. For this purpose, an employer is obliged to consult with the representative labour union or an employee representative, as well as with the National Labour Authority in writing, on all material aspects of any planned mass dismissal and possible measures for keeping the redundant employees employed.

[272] Nevertheless, neither employees, their representatives, nor the National Labour Authority can block the employer in the course of the process preceding the planned mass dismissal. Thus, their rights and powers in this context are limited to a mere obligation of the employer to consult them. *See* paragraph **[273]**(iv) for more information on mass dismissal.

5.2.4 Termination of the Employment

[273] An employment relationship may be terminated in several ways:

(i) Termination by Agreement.
The employment relationship ends on the agreed date. Such agreement must be concluded in writing. The basis for termination must be set out in the agreement.

(ii) Termination by Notice.
An employer may terminate the employment contract if justified cause exists, which must relate to the working ability of the employee and his/her behaviour. For example, if the relevant employee does not achieve the agreed results or does not have the necessary knowledge and skills to perform the given tasks.

Also, there are other reasons for which the employer may terminate the employment contract, such as if the employee is legally convicted of a crime at the workplace or related to the work and/or if the employee fails to fulfil certain working duties, such as if the employee performs his/her working obligations with negligence and carelessly.

In addition to this, an employer may terminate the employment contract of an employee who does not respect working discipline and, for example, unreasonably refuses to perform the orders of the employer or comes to work under influence of alcohol or other drugs during working hours.

(iii) Mandatory Termination of Employment.
Mandatory termination of employment shall occur:
- if it is determined in the manner set out in the law that an employee has suffered a loss of ability to work;
- if pursuant to a court decision or decision of another body, an employee is forbidden to perform particular work and other work is unavailable;

- if, due to serving a prison sentence, an employee is to be absent from work for more than six months;
- if an employee is sentenced to security, correctional or protective measure with a duration of more than six months, as a result of which measure he/she would be absent from work; or
- in the event that an employer ceases to operate (e.g., liquidation).

(iv) Termination by Mass Dismissal.
An employer is obliged to provide a redundancy programme if it determines that, due to technological, economic or organizational changes, a need for the following number of employees employed for an indefinite period of time will cease to exist within thirty days:
- ten employees employed by an employer having more than 20 and less than 100 indefinite-term employees;
- 10% of employees employed by an employer having at least 100 and not more than 300 indefinite-term employees;
- thirty employees employed by an employer having more than 300 indefinite-term employees.

Such a redundancy programme is also required from an employer who establishes that at least twenty employees will become redundant within a ninety-day period due to the reasons stated above, regardless of the total number of employees employed by such employer.

An employer is obliged to negotiate with employee representatives regarding the measures which could avoid mass dismissal with the aim of placing employees in any of the employer's other workplaces. For this purpose, an employer is obliged to inform the relevant employee representative in writing of all material aspects of the mass dismissal and submit a copy of such written information to the National Labour Authority. At the same time, the employer must submit a written report to both the National Labour Authority and the relevant employee representatives on the outcome of negotiations with employee representatives.

However, the employer may expand, in its internal labour regulations, as well as in the employment agreements concluded with the employees, the list of reasons which may represent a breach of the working duties, and such breaches of the working duties represent a legal basis for the termination of the employment by the employer.

(v) Wrongful Termination.
In the case of wrongful termination of employment by an employer, an employee is entitled to file a lawsuit for annulment of such termination within sixty days. As a result of such lawsuit, the employee may be returned to work (so-called reinstatement) and compensated for damage caused to him/her as a result of the wrongful termination. Employees are entitled to a severance payment only in the case of the termination of employment due to redundancy.

As a general matter, it is not possible to derogate from the aforementioned entitlements to the detriment of employees, irrespective of the informal category to which they belong (white-collar workers, blue-collar workers, etc.). The minimum of entitlements envisaged under the Labour Law must be respected in each employment agreement and any provisions that provide otherwise would be null and void.

5.2.5 Labour Costs and Working Conditions

[274] Please note that the minimum net salary prescribed in Serbia for the period of January–December 2023 is RSD230 net per working hour (approximately EUR2).

[275] As for the general working conditions, full working hours are forty hours per week and the daily thirty-minute break is included in the daily working hours. The minimum vacation entitlement is twenty days per calendar year and employees are entitled to additional paid leave in certain situations (e.g., marriage, birth of child, death of immediate family member, voluntary blood donation). Also, employees are entitled to at least 65% of their average daily salary paid in the last twelve months for each day of sick leave.

[276] In Serbia, it is not common for companies to have collective agreements in force. This is due to the fact that the influence of trade unions in Serbia is quite weak and they do not represent a strong force in the process of defending employee rights. As already noted above, the strongest trade unions exist within companies which were historically state-owned.

5.3 Pensions

[277] The Law on Pension and Disability Insurance regulates the scheme of obligatory retirement and social contributions that each employer in Serbia pays on top and in relation to employee salaries.

[278] At the moment, the aggregate amount of salary-related taxes and contributions is equivalent to approximately 60% of the employee's net salary and such taxes and contributions are borne by employers either as their own obligation or on behalf of employees. However, it is important to note that the current framework for subsidies applicable to new investments provides that employers may be entitled to exemptions from such taxes and contributions under certain conditions.

[279] In addition to the mandatory pension scheme, employers are allowed to set up a private pension scheme, i.e., to pay the so-called voluntary pension contributions into one of several private pension funds that operate in Serbia. However, this is still rather rare in practice, partially because this possibility was introduced only a few years ago. These are mainly companies whose shareholders are foreign entities and the beneficiaries are typically members of their top management in Serbia. Also, pension schemes in such cases are often developed on the group level.

5.4 Retention of Key Management and Employees

[280] The Serbian legal framework does not provide for any provisions that would ensure the retention of the key members of the management team or other key employees. However, the relevant management incentive plans may be adopted and be part of the transaction documents. Individual employees may be subject to bonus schemes, which schemes depend on the future performance and business results of the company in question. Also, bonuses for staying at the same working places when the change of the ownership structure of the company occurs may apply in certain cases.

[281] In general, it is possible and common in practice to impose the so-called post-contractual non-competition clauses on vendors and/or key employees, but they need to be limited to a certain territory and to a period which cannot be longer than two years. Please also note that it is mandatory to pay compensation if the post-contractual non-compete duty was agreed upon with an employee (otherwise, such clause is null and void). As for whether this is practicable and enforceable, please note that it is sometimes rather difficult in practice to prove the damages incurred by the breach of the non-compete clause.

5.5 Treatment of Foreign Employees

[282] There are generally no prohibitions against foreigners becoming executives or employed otherwise in Serbian companies. Also, applicable rules typically do not require the presence of Serbian citizens on such boards. However, according to the Banking Law, at least one member of the board of directors and executive board of a Serbian bank needs to be fluent in the Serbian language and reside in the territory of Serbia. In any event, it is prudent to include at least one or a few local members in the companies' management bodies for practical reasons, such as enabling the company to execute day-to-day activities.

[283] Except in the case of company directors who can conclude so-called management contracts, foreigners are required to have standard employment contracts with a Serbian company. The same rule applies to domestic employees (i.e., Serbian nationals).

[284] In order to be able to conclude an employment contract, the foreign national must first obtain a visa for temporary residence (i.e., Visa D) issued by the relevant embassy or consulate of the Republic of Serbia or a temporary residence approval issued by the nearest police department in Serbia for those foreigners who are already staying in Serbia. At the same time, the employers must file a request for the so-called labour market test with the National Labour Authority in order to check whether there are any registered unemployed persons who meet the required qualifications for the relevant job. After the temporary residence permit is obtained and the National Labour Authority confirms that there are no registered unemployed persons on the market who qualify for the relevant job, the employer may apply for a work permit, which is valid for a period that is not longer than the duration of the Visa D or temporary residence approval. The whole process usually lasts between thirty and forty days, so it must be planned in advance before the planned hiring date. As of 1 April 2021, it is possible to apply for a temporary residence permit electronically while the foreigner is still abroad. However, please note that there are still some technical difficulties which may occur when applying electronically for a residence permit.

[285] Visa D or temporary residence approval are issued for a period of up to one year and such period may be subsequently extended, provided that a renewal application is filed at least thirty days prior to the expiry of the current Visa D or temporary residence approval. A holder of Visa D or the holder of temporary residence approval is obliged to notify the local police department/precinct of any change of address of his/her residence in Serbia.

[286] As already noted above, company directors (i.e., this does not apply to supervisory board members) may conclude so-called management contracts instead of standard employment contracts with their respective companies. In the case of foreigners, the conclusion of such contracts is not preceded by a requirement to obtain a work permit; however, such director may still apply for temporary residence approval in case he is planning to reside in Serbia. Please note that the filing fees related to work permits do not exceed EUR200 and such filings are usually made with the help of local lawyers.

[287] A foreign employee is taxed in Serbia for his/her Serbian-sourced income. A foreign employee is taxed in Serbia for his/her worldwide income if he/she becomes a Serbian tax resident (based on the duration of his/her residence in the country or if the centre of his/her life and economic interests is in Serbia). Namely, if a foreigner resides for at least 183 days on the territory of Serbia in a twelve-month period, he/she becomes a Serbian tax resident.

[288] Please note that Serbia has concluded a number of intra-state agreements on social insurance which allow for, *inter alia*, the tax exemption of relevant foreign employees within the first twenty-four months of their stay in Serbia or, as in some cases, even longer than that (e.g., sixty months in case of China).

[289] All the statutory taxes and social contributions (such as pension, health and contributions for non-employment) that apply to employees who are Serbian citizens apply to foreign employees, as well. As already noted above, they amount to approximately 60% of the relevant employee's net salary.

5.6 Director's Responsibilities

[290] It is a relatively onerous responsibility to be a director of a Serbian company. For example, a director may have civil law liability for damage incurred by the company and/or its members/shareholders, as well as third parties (under certain conditions). Also, a director may be obliged to pay certain fines if he/she commits a commercial or petty offence. Finally, the criminal liability of a director may be triggered in certain situations.

[291] Some of the Serbian insurance companies offer liability insurance for company directors. This insurance covers financial damages incurred by third parties by certain acts of directors. However, the Serbian Company Law provides for a possibility that the company may withhold its request for compensation of damages from the director if such decision is made by votes of present shareholders present at the general assembly meeting and if the shareholders who have at least 10% of the share capital are not voting against such decision.

6 ACCOUNTING TREATMENT

6.1 Format and Content of Group Accounts/ Implementation of IFRS

[292] The format of the financial statements and relevant Chart of Accounts (COA) is published by the Ministry of Finance according to the Accounting Law for statistical purposes. As such, it is not aligned with International Accounting Standards (IAS) 1. The same law further prescribes that the framework for preparing financial statements is IAS/IFRS which are translated and published by the relevant National Accounting Committee within the Ministry of Finance. As such, financial statements in Serbia are 'IAS/IFRS-like' but are not completely aligned with IAS/ IFRS. The financial statements explain the general framework for preparation of financial statements (Accounting Law and IAS/IFRS applicable in Serbia) but also list how are those financial statements different from IAS/IFRS (e.g., IAS 1). The reason for the lack of full alignment with other IAS/IFRS could also be the time delay between the adoption of relevant IAS/IFRS by the IAS board and their translation and publication in the Serbian official gazette. In 2016, the Ministry of Finance issued an opinion stating that during the preparation of financial statements for 2016, legal entities that have the ability and the necessary capacity may apply new/revised IFRS since they allow early application, even though they are still not yet translated and published in the official gazette. Legal entities that choose to apply these new/revised IFRS must disclose appropriate information in the notes to the financial statements in this regard.

[293] The general framework for preparation of financial statements is IFRS translated and published by the Ministry of Finance and other laws and regulations which sometimes differ from IFRS (e.g., IAS 1 explained above).

In October 2020, the new Accounting Law was passed, and brought with it changes to the COA and forms of financial statements, which still differ from IFRS. The new Accounting Law was to be applied to financial statements prepared for 2021, which effectively means as of 1 January 2021. In October 2020, the last translation of IFRS was published, containing all the standards that were effective up to that date and which are in use today.

In accordance with the Accounting Law, large entities, parent companies (legal entities that have control over one or more legal entities), public companies, or companies that are preparing to become public, in accordance with the Capital Markets Law, must apply IFRS, whereas small-and medium-sized entities(SMEs) must (or may, respectively) apply IFRS for Small and Medium-Sized Entities (IFRS for SMEs).

Micro and other legal entities, regardless of their size, may apply Rules on the Manner of Recognition, Valuation, Presentation and Disclosure of Positions in the Individual Financial Statements of Micro and Other Legal Persons.

The law provides the possibility of choice. Thus, SMEs may choose to apply either 'full' IFRS or IFRS for SMEs. Also, micro-companies may choose between the Rulebook for micro-companies or IFRS for SMEs or 'full' IFRS. Whichever they choose, standards must be applied continuously for at least five years from the date of the first adoption of chosen standards.

According to the Accounting Law, legal entities are classified as follows:

(i) Micro entities if they do not exceed two of the following criteria:
   - average number of employees is 10;
   - operating income is EUR700 000 in RSD countervalue;
   - average value of operating assets is EUR350 000 in RSD countervalue.

(ii) Small-sized entities, if they exceed two criteria from the previous point but do not exceed two of the following criteria:
   - average number of employees is 50;
   - operating income is EUR8 m in RSD countervalue;
   - average value of operating assets is EUR4 m in RSD countervalue.

(iii) Medium-sized entities, if they exceed two criteria from the previous point but do not exceed two of the following criteria:
   - average number of employees is 250;
   - operating income is EUR40 m in RSD countervalue;
   - average value of operating assets is EUR20 m in RSD countervalue.

(iv) Large entities, if they exceed two criteria from the previous point.

This classification is done by the entity itself on the day of the balance sheet date of the regular annual financial statements, and this information is used for the following year. Newly founded legal entities are classified based on data from financial statements for the year they were founded and for the number of months of operation. Determined information is used for the current year.

[294] As of financial statements prepared for 2021, according to the Accounting Law, groups of legal entities must also be classified by size, as follows:

(i) groups shall be classified as small-sized groups if they comprise the parent legal entity and subsidiaries that are within the consolidation group and which, on a consolidated level, do not exceed two of the following criteria:
   - average number of employees is 50;
   - operating income is EUR8 m in RSD countervalue;
   - average value of operating assets is EUR4 m in RSD countervalue.

(ii) groups shall be classified as medium-sized groups if they are not small-sized groups and they comprise the parent legal entity and subsidiaries that are within the consolidation group and which, on a consolidated level, exceed two criteria from the previous point, but do not exceed two of the following criteria:

- average number of employees is 250;
- operating income is EUR40 m in RSD countervalue;
- average value of operating assets is EUR20 m in RSD countervalue.

(iii) groups shall be classified as large groups if they comprise the parent legal entity and subsidiaries that are within the consolidation group and which, on a consolidated level, exceed two criteria from the previous point.

This classification is done by the parent legal entity itself on the day of the balance sheet date of the regular annual consolidated financial statements. Determined information is used for the current year.

6.2 Possibility of Different Accounting Treatments

[295] The local Serbian accounting framework regarding business combinations (which are defined as transactions in which the acquirer obtains control of another business) is fully aligned with IFRS 3. As such, all identified business combinations must be accounted for using the acquisition method.

[296] As per the business combination definition of IFRS, a 'true merger' or 'merger of equals' is also considered a business combination where an acquirer has to be identified, i.e., no option is possible. Criteria for using merger accounting are determined by IFRS 3 (fully translated and applied in Serbia). Application of IFRS is prescribed by the Accounting Law.

6.3 Application of Merger Relief/Changes in the Assets or Liabilities

[297] If the acquisition is defined as a business combination falling under IFRS 3, there is no merger relief available.

[298] For the events that occur after the event date due to changes in circumstances and availability of additional information, the fair value adjustment of consideration is treated as measurement period adjustment and the contingent liability and goodwill are re-measured. This is effectively a retrospective adjustment and is rather similar to adjusting events under IAS 10 (Events After The Reporting Period).

[299] There is a prescribed mandatory valuation of all identifiable assets and liabilities (fair value at acquisition date) except for leases and insurance contracts, certain contingent liabilities, assets and liabilities measured under other IFRSs (like IAS 12 Income Taxes, IAS 19 Employee Benefits, IFRS 2 Share-Based Payment and IFRS 5 Non-Current Assets Held For Sale and Discontinued Operations, Reacquired Rights and Indemnification Assets). As such, the acquirer's intentions are not relative to the valuation.

6.4 Scope for Provisioning/Goodwill

[300] Per IFRS 3, the costs associated with the transaction are fully expensed and do not form part of the fair value of the consideration.

[301] The goodwill is measured and tested for impairment at least annually and in cases when there are indications of impairment. There is no goodwill amortization.

6.5 Life of Acquired Goodwill (or Goodwill Arising on Consolidation)

[302] The company measures the useful lives of intangible assets. The goodwill and intangibles with indefinite useful life should be tested at least annually (and when factors causing impairment appear) for impairment. There is no amortization charge. In addition to this, it is mandatory to undertake impairment reviews at least annually and when there are indications of impairment.

6.6 Recognition and Amortization of Intangible Assets

[303] Intangible assets are recognized as any other assets, that is, if they meet the criteria of the asset definition from the International Accounting Standards Board (IASB) Framework.

[304] An asset is a resource controlled by the entity as a result of past events and from which future economic benefits are expected to flow to the entity (IASB Framework).

[305] There are both options depending on the intangible asset. Some depreciable amounts of intangible assets are amortized over estimated useful life and others are tested for impairment at least annually and when indication of impairment exists.

6.7 Treatment of Negative Goodwill

[306] Following a business combination (acquisition), extraordinary gain is recorded in P&L. There is no recognition of negative goodwill.

6.8 Treatment of Acquisition Costs

[307] The acquisition-related costs the acquirer incurs, including advisory, legal, and other professional or consulting fees, are to be accounted for as expenses in the periods in which the costs are incurred and the services are received, with one exception. The costs to issue debt or equity securities shall be recognized in accordance with IAS 32 and IFRS 9.

6.9 Effective Date of Acquisition

[308] The effective date of acquisition from which profits of the target company(ies) are brought into the acquiring company's P&L account is the date the acquirer obtains control of the acquired, which is usually the specified closing or completion date of the business combination. Control is further defined as the power to govern the financial and operating policies of an entity so as to obtain benefits from its activities.

6.10 Evaluation of Consideration Payments

[309] The fair value of consideration is measured at the acquisition date. If, following the acquisition, there are additional events and information which change the fair value of the consideration (post-acquisition payments), then the re-measurement of the consideration involves re-measurement of goodwill, and as a result, the original goodwill figure is adjusted.

6.11 EBITDA/Differences Between 'Extraordinary Items' and 'Exceptional Items'

[310] Please note that Earnings Before Interest Taxes Depreciation Amortization (EBITDA) is not defined in accounting standards or accounting laws. As such, the EBITDA definition is subjective and varies between different transactions. In the case of Serbian local regulations, there are no differences between extraordinary and exceptional items. In practice, these 'one-off and non-recurring' items are shown below the EBITDA line.

7 FUTURE DEVELOPMENTS

[311] The overall M&A activity seems to have seen a relative increase in the Q2–Q3 of 2021, with the ongoing mergers of several Serbian banks and banking groups, which continues the existing trend of consolidation of the Serbian banking sector. Further M&A activity in the banking sector is to be expected. Further, a potential for M&A activity can be seen in some other sectors as well, such as IT, agriculture, food production, renewable energy production and others.

[312] Privatization process in Serbia is still not completed. At the moment, the privatization process is within the competence of the Ministry of Commerce. Although the majority of the companies that are currently in privatization are probably not so attractive to potential investors due to massive debts and outdated technology, a number of companies will likely attract potential buyers. Some of these companies are in the agriculture, chemicals and spa sectors. In addition, the process of sale of state-controlled shares in Petrohemija, a state-owned chemical industry complex, has entered into its final phase, and the Sale and Purchase Agreement with Naftna Industrija Srbije, which was the only bidder, is expected to take place in December 2021.

[313] All in all, the M&A trends in Serbia for the short and medium term will depend, on one level, on the improvement of regional and international economic climate and situation in relation to the COVID-19 pandemic, while on the other level, it will depend on the Serbian Government's ability to substantially improve the general economic and legal climate. Serbia has already stated its ambition to become a regional leader and hub for many international businesses that consider operating in Central Eastern Europe (CEE). This ambition will have to be matched with the readiness to cope with many difficult structural problems of the Serbian economy and society, as well as the ability to work diligently on the upgrade and expansion of the existing outdated infrastructure.

www.ingramcontent.com/pod-product-compliance
Lightning Source LLC
Chambersburg PA
CBHW071352230926
51846CB00002B/526
9789403530086